VIOLATED

By

Guitele Jeudy Rahill

Back Cover Photo by Thomas A. Rahill
Editor: Henri Forget

1stBooks - rev. 11/16/01

Violated is a work of fiction. The scenes involving animal cruelty, emotional & sexual abuse occur in dysfunctional families across all cultures and are not at all unique to the Haitian community.

Thank you.

Guitele J. Rahill

ABOUT THE BOOK

Violated is a story of hope deferred. It is the story of what happens when the attempt is made to purchase and possess the human spirit. It is a story which spans three generations of Haitian women. *Violated* sheds light on the disenfranchisement of the women of Haitian bourgeoisie, and the often necessary betrayal of their poorer sisters. It divulges a new perspective on the legacy of incest and intimidation. It captivates and forces the reader to be a reluctant if yielding player in the drama that is the paradox of life in Port-au-Prince. *Violated* pulls the reader into a staggering union with the revered and often feared spirits of Haitian voodoo.

There are some people who say that a dragonfly can see more colors than humans can. Henri Berceuse tried hard to occupy himself with trying to imagine what those colors were. It was unimaginable. As he paced up and down the dry, cracked sidewalk in downtown Port-au-Prince, he thought it was very much like understanding the women he knew. An impossible task, much like trying to imagine the color of air. He puffed out his chest, both from exertion and personal pride. He sighed, slowing his pace to an almost stand still as he looked around at the paradox which was downtown Port-au-Prince.

A figure brushed past his sudden pause. Henri looked up to see a woman wearing a colorful hair scarf as a shield against the sun. She gracefully balanced a large round tray of woven straw on her head. He envied the apparent strength which he discerned from a glimpse of her damp sable neck. The woman dipped and swayed under her load of grilled nuts, colorful candies, and tiny packs of chocolates. Her thin glistening arms were held out lightly yet resolutely to each side. Her small strong hands were laced with conspicuous veins. One might have thought she promenaded the best runways of Europe's fashionable world of haute couture instead of the hot concrete and charcoal streets of hazy Port-au-Prince. Her form and figure displayed no shame in her task, but tenacious determination.

He called out to her, "Aye, psst...*marchande!"*

She continued, seemingly oblivious to his call, and he followed, frowning. Perhaps it was some transient change in her stride which revealed that she'd heard him over the din of Port-au-Prince at midday.

Henri sensed her annoyance at stopping for one who might not be really interested in making a purchase. It was a task for her to set down, unload, reload, and then to resume her pace. He told himself that she belonged to a class which he preferred to pretend did not exist unless he needed them to elevate his own status.

He heard the bleating of a goat from somewhere nearby. Cars honked repeatedly on either side of the narrow dirt street as they rushed recklessly along without traffic signals to control their coming and going. During rainy season, an occasional vehicle would plunge into the ravines which hug both sides of the treacherous roads without interrupting the tempo. *La mize...* Misery... that too was an essential and even anticipated part of life for the Haitian poor.

They shared this space with other *marchandes,* vendors, laborers, various animals, and the diverse ingredients which are an essential part of life in the capital city. Each member of this concert orchestra knows its part and plays it skillfully, unconsciously maintaining timely step in this vigorous dance. *"Aye, Madame!"* Henri called louder, picking up his own pace to end up blocking her further progression.

He always relished interacting with the *marchandes*. Sometimes, he would be thrilled to recognize a girl from his old neighborhood. He was always eager to let them know how well he'd done for himself and he laughed loudly and expansively at their expressions of shock once they recognized him. He took advantage of those chance meetings to ask about many people he hadn't thought about in years.

Averting her eyes from his own after a transient scrutiny, she distinguished him as her social superior despite their identical skin color. Henri, for his part, did not know the young woman before him. He felt he could now easily handle her condescendingly without constraint or remorse. Raising his voice one notch to a higher pitch, he affected the affable manner of someone who counted upon and agreed to be cheated. He leisurely completed his purchase of two tiny boxes of Chiclets. Henri watched her drop the two dirty pennies into some secret and bottomless vault which such women always seemed to carry within their brassieres. After an exaggerated thanks to which she did not reply, he waved her away. This time it was he who failed to make eye contact with her as he realized that she had not even bothered to set her load on the ground before him. She'd merely crouched at the knees, seeming not to care which of the sweet things he chose nor even whether he paid. He winced as he acknowledged that she'd found him to be an intrusion. Only when she'd taken three or four steps away from him did she resume her steady tempo.

She was once again a queen and her realm was the street.

Henri, in turn, realized she had dethroned him as he entered this transaction.

Outside his Cine Royal, Henri emptied both tiny boxes of gum into his mouth as he reflected on the events which had preceded his brisk exit to the noisy pavement. He knew that inside the theater, his wife, Nadege, scurried about the business of managing the cine.

While not a beautiful woman, she carried herself in that regal fashion indicative of the Haitian bourgeoisie. She spoke her French fluently. Nadege Berceuse was a true *bourgeoise*, and in fact, had been born into a family of means. She facilitated Henri's wavering acceptance into that class, making him more palatable to those who were less *nouveau-riche* than he. She had mocha brown skin and straight black glossy hair. In her visage shimmered the vestigial traces of Indian tribes which had inhabited Haiti prior to Columbus. She might have been the historical queen Anacaona herself, but she was plain and insecure. Adding to her feelings of insecurity was a bothersome stutter that seemed to plague her at the most inopportune moments. Henri's money gave her the confidence she needed, and so they were symbiotically and inextricably bound, she the pearl to his oyster.

Henri's mistress, Bernadette, was the cine cashier. She was a *mulatresse* and reaped her confidence from her tenuous status as a woman of mixed descent. She had argued with Madame Berceuse only moments earlier. This was a bother to Henri, as he'd had to mediate between the two women again. Madame Berceuse had accused Bernadette of pilfering funds and had threatened to fire her. Bernadette had defended herself evenly in French, going so far as to strike out at Nadege with some stinging Creole curses that would cause even the stoutest *vagabond* to cringe. Nadege had cried and left the room when her anger and helplessness had resulted in more stuttering than she could control.

Bernadette could be so cruel! She'd actually seemed to enjoy Nadege's discomfort and knew that the latter had left the room to avoid hearing what they all knew to be true. With angry green eyes flashing, she had seemed perched on the brink of adding to Nadege's misery by openly disclosing her relationship with Henri. Had he imagined this? *Dieu du ciel!* (God in Heaven!)

When Nadege had left the room, Bernadette had lowered her eyes demurely and continued her barrage of comments concerning his "stammering and frigid wife." She reiterated her feelings that she would be the best spousal support for Monsieur Berceuse. She reminded him, perhaps for the hundredth time, that a divorce would liberate her to help launch him into true aristocracy. Henri, for his part, considered himself a man of honor. He refused to divorce Nadege. Besides, his associates could more easily accept his *petits indiscretions*, if they didn't end in divorce or scandal.

Henri thought of his three young daughters and swore that even his own loins had betrayed him by spewing forth more women to encumber his life. He sighed, thanking God that they were still young enough to keep the family cook, maid, laundress, and chauffeur engaged while he and Nadege managed the Cine Royal and their newest acquisition, the *Cine Citadel*. Business was excellent.

Now, as he slowly paced, he felt free to explore his indignation at the scene which had taken place inside the theater just before he had sought refuge from the steamy sidewalk. That Nadege still could not accept his having mistresses as a right which he'd earned along with his money was exasperating. Henri, at least, was doing his part as a provider and as a successful businessman. He financed all the household expenditures from his children's private education, to frequent lavish *fetes*.

It was a quirk of his that he preferred his mistresses to be as light complexioned as possible, and from the lowest social class. They were easily impressed by his money, so his very black skin did not matter. They called him *"Monsieur."* Their pretty brown eyes, looking anywhere but directly into his own, showed the accustomed sign of respect to him as their social better.

Yes, he prided himself on his discretion. Henri chuckled to himself because he knew that any scandal with him might cause the others' wives to question slight inconsistencies in their own husbands' conversations.

Nadege, on the other hand, seemed to regard him solely as her provider. She took for granted all the hired help. She expected money to be available for all the best that life could afford. That had always been a part of her life. Once, as Henri proudly summarized his strengths as a provider, she'd raised her eyebrows and had actually said she felt nauseated. It was a disgrace to discuss money. He was to earn it, and the family was to spend it. That was the extent of it. After all, wasn't she managing the maids adequately? His clothes were always crisply washed and ironed. His meals were always beautifully prepared and presented!

So, he continued his relentless search for the one beautiful woman who would love as well as appreciate him. He doubted that such a creature existed, but the hunt for her kept him alive. There was not a great thrill in the search. Instead, he was compelled by an instinct to live life to its fullest, just as he'd drunk the cup of misery to the dregs whenever it had been presented to him.

This latest spat between Bernadette with her fiery green eyes and *Madame* Berceuse had been difficult. He would have to fire Bernadette soon. There was no question about it.

He would set about actively seeking his next *malheureuse,* or poor girl. That was not a difficult chore. Troublesome, but not difficult. So far, he had impregnated at least one of his many mistresses, but those matters were always easily taken care of with an extra 50 *gourdes* to the family. An additional 150 *gourdes* had been sacrificed to a local *boko* who knew just the right combination of herbs and roots to destroy a developing fetus. Still, he worried that someone of consequence might find out about that nasty affair. And now, Bernadette had become so possessive that she was insisting he divorce Nadege. The alternative would be to publicize their liaison to the friends of Port-au-Prince *societe.*

In a nation where appearances were the sum total of possible outcomes, one worked hard to control the former, and tentatively hoped for the latter.

Henri chewed angrily through the gum in his mouth. How could he remove Bernadette from the cine without alienating her? She fancied herself in love with him! Damn women. First one had to work like hell to possess them; then getting rid of them was nearly impossible. Why couldn't they think as progressively as him?

While he did not consider himself a poet, he was a rational man. He was also a man of some imagination, and he believed deep down in his heart in the existence of God. That he believed this Creator was best addressed formally and in French was inconsequential. French was the *lang achte,* the purchased language for those who could afford a formal education. It was more powerful than Creole and therefore more appropriate for a powerful man addressing a more powerful Being. It never occurred to him to worship this Creator.

He did believe, and he often rhetoricized along with his Catholic catechism, that the different areas of the heart had been created so that a man could have room for more than one woman in his heart.

He never questioned the wide leap from the structure of the physical organ to his own motivation. He simply knew it. He espoused it.

These relationships with his mistresses were and could only be business. Their looks and their attention were what he sought; for while he was in their bright arms, while he kissed their yellow breasts and their pink lips, he'd forget the blackness of his own skin and all its implications for him and others like him. Henri had determined long ago, with the American occupation of Haiti between 1915 and 1934, that he would do all he could to escape his blackness and the poverty it seemed to oblige. He fought valiantly against an intrusive memory, but it kept coming back.

The year was 1918. Haiti had had little to do with World War I save for minor civil unrest within the country itself. Henri had been on his way home from school. He'd watched in horror and disgust as an American soldier sodomized a hungry and sweating boy no older than himself. This was not the first time he had witnessed this, and the scene before him seemed to make the stygian sun above even more infernal.

Some of these boys were children whose parents could not afford their education and thus their refuge in a schoolhouse. Still others had no parents at all and had been cast out to the streets by relatives who could barely feed their own children. They were the young beggars of Port-au-Prince.

These young orphans had always been there, for as long as Henri could remember. They would do somersaults or sing, and then stretch out their hands for pennies or for a piece of whatever you were eating. They always disappeared from the streets before dark.

No one, unless he was up to some meanness, could be found on the streets after dark. Darkness was the dwelling place of evil and its servants.

The boys would be compensated with the pennies that could purchase chunks of cassava bread with a thin layer of peanut butter, and if they were lucky, a sprig or two of bitter watercress would be added to this modest but quickly devoured feast. And so, spitting wretchedly, they would hitch up ragged, worn shorts and would limber off like slinking dogs. They saw no one around them and silent witnesses pretended they were invisible. They never heard the "Tsk, tsk" of *the few who noticed their deeds. They heard only the sound of shiny new coins in their pockets. That sound was associated with one more day that they would get to eat a meal. One less day of the wracking, churning and twisting abdominal pain that was hunger.*

Why was this tolerated! Henri imagined that what the boys were experiencing was both humiliating and painful, and he spit in disgust, even as he watched them spit. The soldiers were white and sporting uniforms. Both factors were indicators of unquestioned authority on the small island. The young ones were black and in Haiti. That, simply, was why passersby pretended not to notice.

No one would care. If you were black and poor in Haiti, you were on your own.

Well, Henri was black, but he would not be poor all his life. He would work and do whatever he could to change what seemed to be his destiny.

He had noted that after the soldiers had returned home, the boys would pose, flexing muscles for any white male tourist who cast an eye their way. They'd become accustomed to being called "My sissy" and had taken to teasing any less than masculine male with the term "*masisi*," a term which would lead the most passive Haitian heterosexual male to wield a machete.

As the unbidden memory drew to an end, some unconscious changes stole across his visage. He removed his crisply starched and perfumed handkerchief from his shirt pocket and slowly patted his forehead.

His lips were pursed tightly. Certainly passersby would know that while he was not aristocracy, he was educated and was a man of means. His mid-section sported the girth which proclaimed opulence and was the goal and envy of the poorer Haitians who would flatter him with their clamors of *"Monsieur."* Henri acknowledged that he was not a handsome man, but he was not monstrous by any means. Above all, he had class. He knew how to treat his women and he knew how to be discreet.

Henri did not have true friends. He knew it, and his paramours knew it. He paid dearly for the company he kept, and they were mostly mulatto Haitians of French, Arab, and Spanish lineage.

When he parted from them and went home to look in the mirror, he was often surprised at the unattractive black man whom he found staring back from the glass. Still, he allowed himself to relish in the acquaintances which he had so dearly purchased, even at his own expense. Henri was rich by international standards amid the now poorest nation in the western hemisphere. That was a fact which he accepted easily and without remorse. He had earned the right to help himself to all the privileges afforded the bourgeoisie, including a wife, children, mistresses, excesses in food and other pleasures. A student of philosophy, Henri fancied himself a Sophist, full of knowledge and clever in debate. He was an Epicurean, and even the knowledge which he constantly sought was a source of pleasure for him. A plebeian, he would never be again, and Bernadette would not be allowed to squelch his efforts.

He needed to fire her, but he feared her temper. Capable of unbridled rage, she might set fire to the cine, or God forbid, to his home. He feared the ugly scandal, the inevitable sequelae to Bernadette's frequent rages.

Deep down Henri was painfully aware of his true motives for avoiding this action. Bernadette was far from his equal in the ability to speak French or in financial security. But, he reflected, her amber skin and feline eyes gave her an edge over his money and education even among his own acquaintances.

Henri cursed himself for having introduced Bernadette into his inner circle of *friends*. Yet, her gregariousness, coupled with her greed to obtain all that she felt was her due as a *mulatresse* had jetted her into absolute popularity with everyone she had met. This did not prevent the wives from tossing their heads, and slicking back their straight ponytails as they wrinkled their noses distastefully when Bernadette was not looking their way. But, they admired her nerve and they feared her audacity.

Among the women, Bernadette was never afraid to be vulgar, and she could drink as much as the men did. She told the dirtiest jokes, and the ladies would *pshaw* and avert their glances in shame, while their eyes teared as they both laughed at the jokes and cried for themselves. Bernadette could take away their only security, their men. They would not support Henri. They were too afraid of Bernadette as a threat to their own marriages. Let her amuse herself with Henri for the time being, since he considered her disposable anyway. He would soon grow tired of her and she would be replaced with a new *malheureuse*. Only, they would make sure that Henri's next little tramp knew her place. They would not share their own whispered fantasies and actions as they had with Bernadette. It had been easy to be roped into the role of confessor to inquisitor with Bernadette. One had the feeling that she would always appear as an angel in light of Bernadette's own candidly admitted trysts.

Henri could not count on the men to become involved either. They would all feign ignorance of the matter. They could not risk having Bernadette expose their own secret *liaisons* with her.

Pacing during the hot and humid afternoon had caused Henri to become short of breath. He patted his chest and reflected that this matter might easily cause a delicate and civilized man such as himself to suffer a heart attack and die. It was then that the inspiration came. He would have Nadege fire Bernadette!

It seemed so simple, that he was amazed he hadn't thought of it months earlier. He would wait a couple of days, and then casually mention to his wife, *"My dear, you may have been right about that Bernadette Dubois. I simply hope that she has not helped herself to more cash than you have suspected."*

And then, to further motivate Nadege to swift and merciless action, he would add nonchalantly, *"By the way, cherie, you haven't had her to the house ever, have you?"*

Leave enough to the imagination, and Nadege would take care of the dirty work.

He would continue, *"Of course, this matter might best be settled between you two women. As her employer, I could really destroy the poor girl, and it would of course be to her advantage if I can provide a reference or recommendation for her for a future job."*

Nadege would understand immediately that he intended to maintain his contact with Bernadette outside of their business relationship. This would assuage the embarrassment felt by Nadege, and she could deny to her friends that the whole matter ever happened. *"After all,"* she would say to her friends, *"The poor girl was obviously deluded. If there had ever been a relationship between her and Monsieur Berceuse, he would have never asked me to relieve her of her duties at the cine."*

The topic of conversation would then switch to some more bearable topic such as ballet or one's next trip abroad.

Henri was suddenly jolted back to the hot sidewalk where he had inadvertently stopped while calculating his next move.

He turned around to face in amazement what he thought was one of the most beautiful creatures he had ever seen. He hardly heard a word of the quick and apologetic words which cascaded from her lips as she hastily attempted to dry off his now soaked jacket with her small damp hands. Slowly, Henri realized what must have happened. When he'd stopped suddenly on the pavement, he'd disturbed the rhythm of the sidewalk and she'd collided into him.

Peggy Pouchot bit her full lips until she tasted blood. She fought back unwanted tears. A girl like her was always warned to watch her step in the city. At night, in Fort National where she lived, families even sang about such dangers by the light of their gas lamps. (Someone would say *"Krik"* and those interested in a story would respond *"Krak")*. There was even a song about a young girl whose parents had sent her to the city to *peze cafe,* or to grind the coffee... She'd been arrested by a *gendarme!*

Peggy Pouchot, personally, had ample reason to fear gendarmes or really anyone in uniform. Two years before, in Port-au-Prince, she'd been approached by a man who had identified himself as a *lieutenant* and had commanded her to follow him. She had done just that. There was no disputing a man who looked so powerful.

It had been six months until her family would see her again. And when she was found, she had gulped down the bitter herbs and teas that had forced a very painful and involuntary miscarriage from her young body.

In a country such as Haiti, no one had dared to ask concerning her whereabouts. The authorities wouldn't have helped. Her family had no money with which to influence them into action. Her mother, Mireille, in fact, had suffered a miscarriage herself, as she spent sleepless nights wondering what might have happened to Peggy.

Mireille, affectionately called *Mimi* when her husband was drunk but still on his feet, bore her daily misery as a matter of course. She considered it her due, and her suffering qualified her as particularly human and especially acknowledged by *Bon Die* (God/ The Master) and his many *lwas* or spirits.

Mimi usually never said much anyway. She'd said even less during those six months. She very seldom even ate what her oldest daughter, Regine scraped up for the younger children. Her feet swelled, and she seemed to vomit continuously, sometimes from hunger, sometimes from some deep source inside of her that felt as if she would give birth to the wretched child through her throat and mouth! It was, to her, a relief when she found herself crouching and heaving late one night to quietly and finally rid herself of that which she knew would be her last child.

Regine had been busy fending for the younger ones and bringing in the urine-stained rags in from outside where they'd been airing in preparation for their bedding that night. She'd had no idea that Mimi also needed her to be or to do anything beyond the already mammoth tasks which she accomplished on a daily basis. It was inconceivable that Mimi could need anyone.

No one ever asked what happened to Mimi's pregnancy, and she didn't expect them to. Mimi never offered any information.

Life and the expected misery dragged on.

No one in the Pouchot family went to school, because even the state schools required uniforms, pencils, paper, books. All these had to be purchased, and purchases could not be made without money.

Mimi's husband, Pepe squandered his money as quickly as he earned it, and so education, as with everything else, would be reserved for others.

Pepe was always gone, traveling throughout Haiti, seeking work as a carpenter or mason. When he was home, he was drunk on *kleren*, the clear, cheap liquor strained from sugar cane. It was an expected tradition when he returned home that he would line up everyone, from the oldest to the youngest. He would then whip them all with a belt which always decorated the wall, an awful reminder that he would return home again. They all accepted, including Mimi, that he was beating them for the times they'd misbehaved in his absence. Mimi, who'd had occasion to taste his hard knuckles along with her own blood, rarely intervened. When she did, it was with a simple wave of her hand, and a barely audible *"Mercy, grace...grace...mercy."* Then, she would retreat to mending some rag or pounding some corn or humming some tuneless hum.

Peggy had always been one to try to make sense out of a situation. She'd searched Mimi's face for some sign that would explain Pepe's seemingly senseless actions. She couldn't remember her mother ever looking her in the eye at those times when she sought some look of understanding or, at the very least, sympathy. So, she had stopped looking at Mimi altogether.

The children would retire to some darker corner of the one-bedroom cement hut and rub at the stinging welts which were reminiscent of the pain. It was never their habit to console each other. They had never seen that done. They had felt only the need for sympathy, but were unable to conceive of empathy. Still, the last one to stop crying or showing pain would inevitably be mocked by the others.

It was a wonder to Peggy that they didn't call the belt "father" because at least they could count on it always being around.

When Peggy had finally found her way home from the dark hovel in which she'd been incarcerated by the *lieutenant,* no one punished her for being gone so long...not even Pepe, although she had braced herself for the assault. Strangely, everyone stopped looking at her too. They sort of spoke towards her when they had to. She assumed it was due to any of numerous beliefs that they held concerning people who suddenly disappeared and then reappeared.

She certainly felt different and older.

Superstitions forbade any discussions of what had happened to her. If she'd been taken by a lougarou or werewolf woman, talking about it might have opened her up as well as those around her to future violations of their souls. If she'd been taken by a *makout*, well, there was the safety of younger and more vulnerable members left in the family to be considered. For her part, Peggy was too ashamed to volunteer any information.

She had seemed okay once everyone ignored her. When she began to be surly and moody a month later, she had been packed off with a clean dress and panties to Mimi's mother and older spinster sister in *La Plaine*. When the younger ones noticed she was not home, the only explanation they had been offered was that Peggy was now *fini*.

Peggy had only been home for six days and now she might be arrested for spilling water on this gentleman!

Henri removed his fragrant handkerchief once more from his breast pocket and feigned inconvenience as he patted the areas of his shirt and slacks which his girth permitted him to reach. "*Mademoiselle*, what have you got on your pretty young mind to render you so careless?"

Peggy became increasingly shocked and dismayed. She felt he was ridiculing her by referring to her as "*Mademoiselle.* After all, she was neither educated nor rich, so she could not be a *Mademoiselle* to him. A man of his class should have referred to her only as a *Ti fi*...a girl. "I would like to take you home," he said and she had never heard such gentleness in another person's voice. "Where do you live?"

She dared a brief glance at his face for a moment and then a dreadful thought quickly caused her to avert her eyes again.

This well-dressed *monsieur* would see where she was living with her mother and eleven siblings! She pleaded that she had left home early that morning shortly after sunrise, and that she was already late in bringing home the bucket of rare and expensive clean water. He insisted that he would get her there much quicker by automobile than her feet could carry her.

She countered with, "But your car will get wet inside. "Don't worry about it, *ma chere,*" Henri responded smoothly. "I have people whose only task it is to care for my car. Now, where do you live?" "*Fort National,* but *Non, merci.* I'm sorry. My mother will beat me if she sees me coming from a man's car...and the neighbors...you know how it is for girls, monsieur. They will talk about my family and say that I have not been properly raised. You have to understand... You must have daughters..."

Henri winced. *"Mais, oui!* I have daughters older than you! How old *are* you, my dear?" He raised his eyebrows in a manner that seemed to Peggy to compel a response. He took advantage of her confusion and propelled her gently but firmly by a soft, cool elbow.

She mumbled, "Sixteen," and then quickly, "But I will be seventeen in October." "You are quite the *jeune dame,"* he teased. "I bet you have many boyfriends." "Oh, *non, Monsieur.* I..."

She hesitated, glancing back, realizing they had abandoned the bucket of water quite a few steps back and were approaching a red convertible parked half on the street and half on the sidewalk.

Sensing her hesitation, he firmly grasped her elbow and placed her in the automobile. Closing the door, he remembered to cast a cautious glance at the cine door before he made his way to the driver's side of the automobile. A look at the dampened cotton shirt clinging to her firm young breasts and he cast all caution to the wind. Bernadette could wait. Nadege would wait.

Peggy sat with her two damp hands folded between her legs, and felt this was not the proper way for a young lady to sit in a gentleman's car and then wondered helplessly just how a young lady should sit in a gentleman's automobile. She felt the small car sink slightly as the large man took his place behind the wheel. Her mouth became dry as she remembered the last time she had been coerced into a car, and she felt a sense of overwhelming panic." Are you certain you are not taken?" he asked. "Taken where, *s'il vous plait*," she responded. He laughed, throwing his head back so that she could see rolls of fat around his neck. "Can you really be that innocent? I am asking if you are being cared for, little yellow bird." "Oui, Monsieur. My mother, Mimi takes care of us the best way she can with what Pepe gives her. My name is Peggy, *s'il vous plait, Monsieur*," she added as an afterthought. "I see," he said slowly, suggesting he saw a lot more than he was admitting. Peggy found that she could not think as fast as his questions warranted. Confused, she chewed on her lower lip, afraid he might ask another question.

Distantly, she heard him saying "You shouldn't bite such lovely lips," and his tone was familiar.

Her heart fluttered wildly and she wondered if he knew just how much she felt like the little bird he kept calling her. "And where is your papa, yellow bird," he continued. "Pepe works hard. He works far from home with some *Blancs* from abroad. Americans, I think." Fearing what he might think of Pepe not being home, she added hastily, "He comes home sometimes." "Of course."

The car raced crazily through the crowded streets of Port-au-Prince, here and there barely missing first another vehicle and then a goat or guinea fowl.

Peggy found it strange to be in such a pretty car instead of dancing to avoid it and the many other elements of Port-au-Prince chaos that threatened those who were pedestrians.

Suddenly they had left the city and entered Fort National, and almost as suddenly she could see the little gray, stone house built in the midst of a nameless cemetery.

Cemeteries in Haiti were never named except after the first individual buried in them. This person was then acknowledged as the *Baron*, an essential figure in Haitian voodoo. Pepe, on one of his drunken excursions had decided to lay a foundation for his home right in the midst of the graveyard, disturbing the *Baron's* bones as a consequence. Subsequently, the Pouchot children had been stricken with various unknown ailments that often threatened their lives. Their neighbors were quick to make signs of the cross and to fondle small blackened bundles of dried and sweat-soaked garlic around their necks as they passed the house.

Mimi, living there with her twelve children was in a constant state of vigilance. She had given up going to *Bokos* for help. She could not afford them. She turned instead to Jesus, whom she heard was free. The only problem was that He made a lot less noise or commotion in her defense than the *lwas* seemed to for their worshippers. Still, Mimi had learned long ago to suffer quietly, and the god of the Protestants seemed to require no more of her than just that, and to hope.

Peggy winced as she noticed her older sister, Regine, cautiously approaching the car. Regine's coarse, black hair was tightly braided, and her face showed signs of acne from the sun and sweat. Absentmindedly, she raised a hand to her own head, and smoothed down a brown-black braid with hands that were still damp. She'd been told that her hair and skin color were her strengths, inherited from a French great-grandfather whom she'd never known. Those same traits, however, often made her the target of Pepe's unbridled rage when he was drunk. He would accuse Mimi of infidelity and yank hard at Peggy's braids as evidence of this.

She sat straight and stiff in the automobile and braced herself for the scorn of those living beyond the graveyard. Cars were not a popular sight in her tiny *lakou*.

Horrified, she saw that her younger brother, Toro, the one born only 4 years after her, also approached. He was twelve years old with black-purple skin and completely naked, his dingle blowing in the breeze. He had long outgrown his one pair of raggedy shorts. He stuffed a chunk of cold corn meal into his mouth and unabashedly approached the automobile.

Everything that had seemed normal before now seemed filthy and embarrassing. Peggy silently wished to die. Then, she didn't dare give in to what she wished as Mimi hurried out, wiping her hands on her skirt and shooshing the kids aside. "*Padon, padon*, children. Can't you see we have *etrange* here?"

The children's curiosity concerning the stranger and the shiny red car were greater than their fear of punishment and they continued to hinder her progress toward the car.

Peggy stumbled out, rushed to her mother, and with a swift kiss on the cheek and a *"Bonjou,"* made herself scarce. She remembered to drag as many of the children behind her as she could. It was not polite for children to listen to the conversation of adults. They were neither to be seen nor heard.

When Mimi finally sat on the one step in front of the house and the car had finished stirring up the dust and bleached rocks, the children all ventured out. No one spoke. They waited. After what seemed like forever, Mimi smacked her thigh loudly and sighed. Nani, the youngest girl, who was two years old, tumbled from the broken step from which she'd perched while sucking a tiny black thumb as she twirled a tiny, dusty braid. She had been about to lean on her mother when the smacking sound occurred and she thought she'd been hit. She screamed loudly, forgotten thumb aloft, banishing the sobriety of the moment.

Mimi heaved Nani up onto her lap and rubbed at her head, although she hadn't noticed the fall or which part of the body had been hurt. "Well, I know some of you might be considered too old, but..."

She waited, sensing their anticipation, and also fearing what she was considering. She looked into their dark limpid eyes and saw upturned faces which revealed little nostrils filled with dust. Nani slowly quieted and began nursing her bruised elbow, while she tolerated the vigorous head rubbing.

Mimi announced, "You'll all be going to school. There'll be money to buy books, pencils, and paper. You'll learn to speak in French." She cast a glance at Peggy, and then looked away. Somehow she didn't feel as excited after looking at her second oldest child. "Peggy went out to buy water and instead brought you all something even better." She looked again at Peggy and appraised her from head to toe and while Peggy shifted uncomfortably, Mimi continued, "Even though she came home without the water and I don't know what we will use to drink..."

Peggy stiffened, expecting a rebuke. When none came, she dared a question. "Is the *Monsieur* going to hire you to do his family's wash?" she ventured. "What?" Mimi answered, looking far beyond the tombstones at her feet. "The wash? *Non, cheri*. He doesn't need *me* for anything. It's you, he needs. He has money and wants more children. You can make beautiful children for any man. You are lucky that way. He will pay your way through school until you speak better French than even Napoleon Bonaparte himself. He will pay for your brothers and sisters to go to school too. He even said he would pay for the uniforms. I think he is a good man."

Peggy wondered who Napoleon Bonaparte was and why it was so important that she learn to speak French better than he, but she could not hear her own voice above all the other children clamoring about wearing socks and shoes, and eating at least once a day. The whole idea of having beautiful children didn't seem so wonderful to her. Any time she'd ever been called beautiful, it had always been followed by something bad. She gaped open-mouthed as Toro did a wild dance, writhing his naked hips and knuckling Nani on the head and was shocked that Mimi laughed instead of cuffing him on the ear. Her breath came in choked gasps.

Mimi turned and walked inside, heaving Nani up by her armpit. As her mother left her view, it never occurred to Peggy that she could dissent.

The next morning, Peggy awoke with the crowing of their scrawny rooster, Prince. Mimi was already outside, halfheartedly sweeping the loose dust back into the graveyard. *"Bonjour, Manman,"* she mumbled, and waited. Mimi stopped what she was doing but did not turn. Peggy made her way around so that she could be in front of her mother. "I'm going to get the water now, *Manman,*" she said with eyes respectfully downcast. "In what bucket, Peggy? And are you too big to kiss me good morning today?" "Non, *Manman*," she responded sheepishly. "What bucket," she echoed as she planted a quick kiss on Mimi's cheek. She noticed that Mimi had taken care to remind her that she'd left their bucket in Port-au-Prince the day before, and braced herself for a tongue lashing. Mimi straightened herself and pressed a hand on the small of her back, groaning. "Go on over to Barnav's house and borrow a bucket from his *Madanm*," Mimi said wearily. "Tell her I will be cooking today and I'll send her a plate. Quickly, before the sun comes up." "Oui, *Manman. Male*. I'm gone."

Peggy was glad she was being sent to Banav's house. She would see Yolette and they could talk about what happened with ...She realized that she did not even know the man's name. She wondered if Mimi did since the two of them talked for so long. Yolette knew about men. She was not afraid of men. She even seemed to like the attention they received from men when they went for water together. She would twist her skinny behind and laugh louder than necessary when what they said was not even funny. She laughed at Peggy because Peggy wouldn't let them touch her. She told Peggy secrets that Peggy excitedly looked forward to hearing.

Yolette did not live far from *Fort National*, but she ran quickly, aware that Mimi was watching her and expecting her to show that she was hurrying. When she felt that she was out of Mimi's view, she slowed down, panting. Shortly, she reached the dilapidated house, and smelled again the raw sewage running in front of it. She saw Yolette step out, and make a tossing motion with a small red and white enamel vase which she carried. She knew that Yolette was adding the previous night's urine to the already steaming accumulation. "*Ey*! Peggy! *Kote ou prale*? Where are you going," Yolette asked vacantly. "To see you, hammer head! I'm in front of your door, *pa vre*? Right?" "Who are you calling hammer head, you yellow *lougarou*," she laughed. Peggy laughed too, despite herself. She liked Yolette. Yolette always made her feel stupid, but she did it in a way that let her know they would always be good friends. "My *Manman* wants to borrow your mother's bucket. I lost hers yesterday." "Tell me, *s'il vous plait*, how you can lose something as big as a bucket when folks have so little to begin with," Yolette said accusingly. "Well, this man made me do it," Peggy began. "What man can make you disobey your mother and leave your bucket behind. Was the bucket empty or had you already bought the water?" Yolette sat on the ground, placing the vase

34

inside the house. Peggy let out a sigh of exasperation. "Never mind what was in the bucket or where the bucket is, Yolette. This is important. *Koute-m*. Listen to me. He made me get into his car and he brought me home." Yolette gave her a questioning look, but didn't interrupt. She knew Peggy well enough to know that something had disturbed her friend. She began to unbraid her own hair, listening intently to what Peggy was saying. "He talked with *Manman-m* for a long time and when he left, Mimi started talking about him paying for me to go to school. She said he will pay for uniforms and everything. And he will pay not just for me for all my brothers and sisters too." "Is your *manman* leaving your Papa for this man? You went after water and brought back a new Papa? What are you saying, Peggy," she persisted as Peggy shook her head vehemently. "*Non, non, non*! That's what I thought at first. Then Mimi said he wants beautiful children, and..." "That's what *I* said! If he wants a baby factory, your *manman* is the one," Yolette teased. "I know, I know, "Peggy said quietly. "Oh, come on! My mother has seven already and she's younger than Mimi. You know I'm playing with you. Anyway, what are you talking about?" "That's the stupid part. Mimi said that this man...I don't know his name...She said that he wants me to have children for him. Yolette,

I don't want children. I'm so busy now with *Mimi's* children. I don't ever want children. They just add to the misery." "Don't say that, Peggy. Haven't you heard that proverb? '*Ti pitit se riches pov malere*'...Children are the riches of the poor.' We should always want children. God gives them to us for.." "Fine, fine! *You* go ahead and have children. Have all the children you want. I hope you feel rich when they're all crying for food and you have none to give them. *Non. Tann.* Wait. Yolette, the thing is I don't know this man. He's married and has three daughters, he said. They might not like me. What if they beat me? They can, you know, because they're rich and I'm poor so they have the right..." "*Egare*! Stupid. Don't you know anything? If this man is married and has children, he is not going to bring you to his house as a *restavek*. The wives of rich men do not tolerate pretty girls in their house. He is going to care for you away from his house. You will be his mistress. Child, I wish I had your clear yellow skin color. I would get a man like that and I would give him more children than a *manman chyen*, a female dog!" "Oh, my God, Yolette. You mean he is going to put me in a house all by myself? I don't want to live all by myself. I don't want to be a mistress. I don't want to ever get married. Why should I live with a man and bear his children? So he can come beat me whenever he wants and mount me whenever he's drunk?" "He won't marry you, don't worry. You said he's already married, right? Okay, then. He can't marry again. He will just use you. It's not that hard. Just stay pretty, and keep yourself clean. You may not even have to cook for him since he is married and his wife will expect him to eat at home. Just don't let her find out about *you*." "Her? Who? His wife? Who is she? What do you mean? My God, I don't even know *his* name!" "Slow down, girl," Yolette laughed again, her unbraided hair now a mass of thick jutting branches. "I'll take him if you don't want him." "Go ahead, and take him. Tell *Mimi* you'll take my place." "Yeah, yeah, he doesn't want my second hand black tail. He wants innocent little you. You know what, Peggy? I don't think I have ever been as innocent as you." "Yolette, what do I tell Mimi? What if he comes tomorrow? Oh, God, what if he comes today!" Yolette reached up and gently pinched Peggy's nose. "Peggy, what can you tell Mimi? Can we ever tell a *gran moun*, a big person what we think? Do they even ask? We were born to misery. Now, *Bon Die* is using you as a way for your family to not be in misery, *pitit*. Just remember who I am when I come before you one day with five or six hungry kids. Now, do you want that bucket?"

"*Oui*. Give me the bucket. My *Manman* is waiting." "*Manman!*", Yolette called out to her own mother! *Peggy vin prete bokit la!*" "Peggy is here to borrow the bucket!" "*Sispann rele pitit! Bali-l, souple*!" "Stop yelling, child. Give it to her, please," came from inside. "*Male*, Yolette. I'm gone," Peggy whispered. "Oh, don't look like you're going to your burial, Peggy. Think of it as the wake if you must be morbid. Remember, there is always food and laughter at a wake! *Babay!*"

Months had gone by before Henri had returned for Peggy. The affair between him and Bernadette had gone as he had planned. She no longer worked at the theater. He had found her employment as a secretary and home aide with a new associate in *La Plaine*. Nadege Berceuse seemed minimally content for the moment and he could now negotiate setting up discrete lodging for him and the young Peggy.

The Pouchot children had long given up hope and had stopped counting the days. They had all thought that he would be back the very next day. Mimi had kept the entire matter from Pepe who had been home for a short week. She told herself that she would have told him, except he just never seemed sober enough to discuss it. Now, she was glad that she had not told him. He would be laughing at her and at her hopes for her family. He would think that she did not trust him to provide for the family and in fact she didn't. But, she had a feeling that if she dared to say this out loud, Pepe would go completely crazy, lining up the children, beating everybody with whatever he could find. No, Mimi was glad she had not told him. She dreaded the ridicule that would accompany his blows even more than the physical sting of his punches.

Peggy felt only relief that the man had not returned and she hoped he never would. She had no idea what the man expected of her beyond bearing children. She knew, from watching and helping Mimi deliver the younger ones how painful childbirth could be; and although Yolette had no idea, she knew how painful sex could be, having being coerced into it. She also remembered bitterly the taste of the brew that had killed the small life inside her after her captivity.

She would have preferred to be any man's washerwoman or his cook rather than his birthing cow. Yes, she was relieved that the *Monsieur* had not returned. Perhaps he had found another young heifer to bear his calves.

Then, on a Sunday afternoon, as Peggy sat shelling Congo beans in the shade of a great big *mapou* tree, she was jerked to attention by an unfamiliar sound. She looked up in time to see the *Monsieur's* car stirring up white dust as he approached her house only a few yards away. Her shoulders sagged woefully. He had come after all. Her heart beat wildly. She felt that she knew what a chicken felt like after you'd slit its throat and dropped it on the ground to bleed to death. She was frozen to the large gray rock on which she sat. She watched the activity around the house as the children jumped and shouted as if Jesus Christ Himself had returned. She heard nothing, only the hissing in her ears. Then, as Mimi pointed to where she sat, she willed herself to stand. Still, she could not move. From where she stood, she sensed, rather than saw him smile at her. She remembered how he had boasted about all the people he had working for him, and knew she would become just another laborer to him. She started toward the house.

So that was it, she thought. She had no bags to pack and nothing to put in a bag anyway. She wiped her right hand on the thin cotton dress that she wore, to remove the dirt from the bean pods. In her left hand, she carried the calabash container with the beans. The pods had been left under the tree for the local goats and pigs. They were not fortunate enough to own any animals beyond their one scrawny rooster.

As Peggy approached the strange man, she was amazed at how familiar he looked. It was as if she had only seen him last the day before. She noted that he was not totally unpleasant looking. He wore a clean white shirt, starched and pressed till it practically shone. "Are you ready?" he asked, scrutinizing her. Peggy did not answer. She felt uncomfortable with his eyes on her. Then again, she did not feel ready. She did not know what to be ready for.

She said, "I have to *pipi*," and then regretted saying that as she felt so foolish. She imagined that a yellow rivulet was snaking its way down her thighs and to her calves. "I didn't hear you, *yellow bird*," he laughed. "Nothing," she said quickly and stood by the car. Mimi, her eyes averted, reached a hand toward Peggy, but Peggy did not know how to react. "The beans," Mimi prompted, and then Peggy realized that this would be a perfunctory good-bye. She wanted to scream out to her *Manman*, "Why are you always sending me away, *Manman*!"

She handed the calabash to Mimi and then looked around at her brothers and sisters. Only little Nani was crying, and Peggy could not be sure why. Nani cried often and no one ever really took notice unless she screamed or unless blood was sighted. "Go in the house, everyone," Mimi said.

Peggy's eyes filled with hot tears as she realized that *everyone* did not and would not ever include her again. The ground wavered through her tears as she stared at it. "I thought you would not come anymore," Mimi said. "I am a busy man, but I am a man of my word, *Madame*."

Peggy decided she should leave them alone. She knew it was a conversation between adults and her presence was a show of disrespect. She slowly made her way to the drying line and took off a clean brassiere and her two underpants. That was all that would fit in the pocket of the dress she wore, anyway.

As she made her way back to where they stood, she noticed that Mimi was tying what appeared to be a small round ball in a kerchief that she wore. This bundle was quickly shoved into the mother's blouse toward her left breast. Peggy had no doubt as to what had happened. She remembered frequent times when she had watched neighbors stuffing wads of money in their shirts after selling a pig. She felt strangely removed from the situation. "Let us go," he said to her, and he started toward the car. Peggy hesitated, looking at Mimi, who waved her away rather than waving at her. "*Manman*..." she began, tremulously. "We did fine," Mimi interrupted. "Oui, *Manman*, but.." "We did fine! All is well," Mimi continued brusquely. "Regine will have to do a lot more now that you are gone, but she is a good girl and she will do her best, so don't worry about her."

Peggy recognized a tone of disapproval approaching anger in her mother's voice and ached for Mimi to look at her instead of toward her. She needed something from Mimi's eyes that she thought could be there if only the mother allowed it. But it was not to be. Mimi had already turned away and begun to walk to where the other children waited. There was work to be done. "*Manman*!"

Peggy thought she had screamed out, but then realized that the cry had been stifled in a pit deep inside her. No one had heard. Something told her that if she repeated it loud enough, the mother would return and a change might be forthcoming. She glanced wildly from the car to the mother's retreating back and then again to the car where the *Monsieur* stood, holding the door for her. She looked one last time at the tiny house and saw the door slamming shut. She feared what she was feeling and she felt guilty as she realized that she was actually angry at Mimi. She walked, like a zombie, to the automobile.

Strangely, and she did not know why, but Peggy wished Pepe had been home.

As Peggy plopped herself into the automobile, her face was hot and she felt herself sobbing. The *Monsieur* pretended not to notice and she was grateful.

Her thoughts danced crazily in her mind. She did not belong in that car. Where was he taking her? She hated automobiles. They either ran you over or you were taken somewhere you didn't want to be in them. She groped in her pocket for the undergarments that she had stuffed there and clutched them tightly and securely. The Monsieur continued to stare straight ahead as he maneuvered the car from Fort National and through the madness that was Port-au-Prince traffic. Peggy felt everything flying past her in a blur.

Finally, she had stopped sobbing and the tears were softly stealing down her cheeks. She felt ashamed of herself. After all, she was a big girl, all of sixteen years old. She quickly bent her head down to her lap, wiping her face with the hem of her dress. She glanced at his profile. No, he was not a good looking man but he was not really ugly. Not like...

He had been quiet so far. She sniffed loudly, so she would not have to sniff repeatedly like a sniveling baby. So he was used to paying for what he wanted. And he wanted her. Maybe more than her own *Manman* even. "So you've stopped," he said. "What, please, *monsieur*?" she sighed. "You've stopped crying. Am I so awful? I am trying to help you and your family. I will not hurt you." "I don't think that you will hurt me, *monsieur*," she responded, full of hurt and pain. "I have a small bungalow set up for you in *Petit Gouave*. There is a nice bed there. You will be very comfortable. I have made arrangements with some local merchants so that you will receive fresh milk, charcoal and peanuts every day. You will not need to pay them any money. Everything is charged to me and I have already paid for a month's worth of provisions for you." "*Merci, monsieur*", Peggy said softly, carefully pronouncing the *"r"* in *Merci* so that he would know she had been exposed to *some* French. "What will I do with all that food? Is there a *tap-tap*, a truck that runs people back and forth near where you are taking me? Can I bring some milk for Nani, please? She is so small and she is often sick. She had the malaria, you know. She needs...someone...to take care of her." "I don't want you to worry about Nani or anyone else. They are well taken care of from now on. I have made sure of that. Your mother will be sent money every month until you are able to finish school and help her yourself, *d'accord*?" "*Oui, Monsieur, merci, Oui.*

45

Peggy decided that this meant she could not freely go and see her family and the tears began to flow again. "What now, yellow bird? You should be happy!"

Peggy wished he did not call her that. After all, birds were for killing and eating. Hadn't she watched her younger brothers using crudely made slingshots to knock birds out of the trees to feed the smaller children? There was not much meat on the scrawny wild birds, but enough for a three or four year old to consider a feast, once properly seasoned and fried. No, she did not want to be a bird! But she would not tell him that. He would find her ungrateful and probably return her home in disgrace.

She resigned herself to her new position. She would clean and cook everyday. She knew he would not be with her everyday, because he had a family. But, she had to always be prepared so she would not be ashamed if he showed up needing his meal. After all, he had paid Mimi for her services. She represented Mimi and could not afford to be returned home in disgrace. She could not risk whatever Mimi had arranged with the *monsieur*. There were the other children to think of. "I am happy, *monsieur*. I see that you are a very good man and that you are very kind to my family."

She thought she did not sound sincere, but she was.

Looking at the relief on his face, she was happy she had said those words.

The automobile stopped in an area surrounded by lush greenery. As she cautiously opened the car door, she noticed a row of small, neat houses. Here and there people sat, leisurely rocking on a front porch. Music could be heard from a tinny sounding radio nearby but the sound was so festive, she almost walked to the beat of the *Konpa* tune. Restraining herself, she followed him past people who saluted him, *"Bonsoir, Monsieur Berceuse,"* echoing behind her and all around her.

Peggy slinked behind him, head bowed. She was ashamedly aware of being watched and she stuck her hands miserably in her pocket to fondle the familiar panties she had balled up in there. She noted that he wordlessly acknowledged all greetings with a casual and noncommittal wave of a hand. "I own these apartments," she heard him saying. "The old man living in the room next to you, he is responsible for maintaining the grounds and the crops that you see. He does not pay rent. He will see that you are furnished with any fruits or legumes that you need without your having to go to market."

As they entered the apartment, Peggy said, "What will *I* do, *Monsieur,* the wash alone? You have someone to do everything else already!"

She wanted to tell him that she hated doing the wash with that caustic chunk of raw soap that she would rub against Pepe's dirty khaki pants. The spaces in between her fingers were raw from rubbing clothes with her hands to ensure their cleanliness so that Pepe would not hurl them at her and demand that they be re-washed.

Henri Berceuse picked up a small gas lamp, trimming the wick, lighting it and replacing the glass shield around it. Only then did he respond to her. He touched her shoulder and leaned to kiss her on the mouth.

His seriousness frightened her and she physically retreated to find herself seating clumsily and suddenly on what her groping hands revealed was a bed behind her. Realizing her discomfort, he stopped his advance. Licking his lips and letting his shoulders drop with disappointment, he said, "You will not need to do anything but be beautiful and take care of yourself."

She looked around, not believing what she'd heard. There was actually a mirror on a dresser up against one wall. While she was in this apartment, she wouldn't have to look at her reflection in a piece of wayward aluminum sheet from a nearby roof. On the dresser, in front of the mirror, was a beautiful brown and clear comb and a brown hairbrush. She had often seen such items at the marketplace and coveted them, feeling sure that she would never own them. There was also a beautiful new clay pot to keep drinking water cold and it was covered with a fitting clay cap.

It was just one room, but there was so much in it! Henri smiled as he watched her take in her surroundings. He exhaled, knowing that she could get used to what he knew were luxuries to her. "I am pleased that you are pleased." "Oui, *Monsieur Berceuse*," she said, tentatively trying what she now knew was his name.

She thought he was ridiculing her. When she dared make eye contact with him, she saw that his eyes were misty. "A nice man," she thought. "I wonder what is wrong with me. I have offended him." Perhaps if she moved closer so that he could try to kiss her again if he wanted...

Abruptly, as if he had been thinking of something else, he said, "Well, I have to go now, my dear. I will return."

She stood, prepared to stand formally as he took his leave. "Beware of the neighbors' wagging tongues. Be careful what you divulge. You are a mere child. If your stomach is patted, be sure you do not vomit up all that you know."

He touched her gently on the shoulder and turned his cheek toward her for a good-bye kiss. "Like a father," she thought, in amazement.

Instead, she stood in front of him and solemnly lifted up her face to him, eyes closed... obediently, he thought as he hungrily met her trembling lips, finally sure that he could possess her. Trembling, Peggy allowed her lips to part as she felt his insistent, searching tongue. Her breathing quickened and she began to feel intense pleasure in her hesitant following of the movements of his tongue. She gasped as he sucked her own tongue and felt her nipples harden. She stifled what would have been a loud moan, afraid she would shame herself. Then, she heard a deep rumble in his throat and she felt what seemed like electrical surges through her womanhood as he seemed to read her mind and squeezed both of her breasts at once. No longer able to stand, she fell back on the bed, yielding sweetly and completely; and Henri felt that if ever there was a heaven, he had found it.

For the first time in her life, Peggy knew sex without coercion and without pain. She felt she could be with this man forever. He seemed to ask nothing of her but to share in his pleasure. She found herself looking forward to telling Yolette about *this* story. Then he was piercing her, with her clothes still on her. Peggy still felt no pain.

Only a mounting pleasure. She held onto his neck, feeling the sweaty rolls behind his neck. Briefly, and quickly he thrust, moaning all the while. He touched her all over and, it felt, all at once. Then, he was screaming out "Oh, yellow bird, yellow bird, sing for me!"

Confused, she removed her hands from his neck and tried to sit up. Then, he collapsed on her, preventing her from sitting up.

Amazed, she looked up at the ceiling. When he raised himself up on his hands, he looked down at her, chest heaving, and what he whispered next startled her. "Home again," he said, kissing her on the nose. "You please me, yellow bird. You have done well."

Then, he was gone. Just like that.

Afterwards, she got up to get water from the faucet outside the house to wash herself. She made sure to avoid the eyes of the *geran*, the man who cared for the property, certain he would somehow guess what she'd been up to inside. *Bon Die*, he probably even heard Monsieur Berceuse's screaming voice!

Giggling, she brought the water in and completed her toilette inside.

Afterward, when he would come over for his quick visits, she would still deferentially avoid eye contact, but she felt herself becoming bolder as his lover, each time learning something from him that she could offer back to him during the next rendezvous... smiling modestly inside when he appeared surprised. Whenever he would visit, he would prove himself a tender and ardent, if selfish lover. He was good at taking care of her food and shelter. She never asked for anything beyond that. He would bring her news from Mimi and the family.

Nani was not as sickly and was even getting a little plump. Toro was going to school and could be found with his nose in his books under the *mapou* tree every day. He was steadfast in his studies. Regine had not been sent to school. With Peggy gone, she was needed around the house.

Mimi had begun a small business in which she would buy sacks of rice wholesale and sell them by the *marmite* to neighbors and passersby who now knew that she had rice and sometimes dry kidney beans to sell. She carefully measured out the tin cans full of rice or beans into her buyers' bags. She prided herself on not padding the bottom of her cans like some merchants. Peggy was gleeful when she received news of home, and Henri seemed happy to relate the information to her. He was such a good storyteller. He made everything sound so funny, even the sad things. "What about Pepe," she asked one day? "That old vagabond! I don't think he even realizes you are not there anymore. When I see him, he is drunk and humming or drunk and cursing. I am his best friend whenever I can drop some change in his hand for his *kleren*." He paused, enjoying her smile. He seldom got the opportunity to see it. "Oh, I have met your friend, Yolette," he continued. "She has, er...convinced me to bring her here one day while you were in school." He spoke faster. "She said she wants to visit you . She wants to surprise you. I took the liberty of throwing her a few *gourdes* to pay for the *taptap* that will bring her here."

Peggy looked at Henri, thoughtfully, when she was sure he had looked away from her. "*Oui, Monsieur*," she answered slowly. "She said you two have always been good friends," he said, she thought almost defensively. "That is correct, *non*?" "*Oui*," she said shortly. "*Oui*," she repeated again quickly, fearing she had been rude. "*Bon*. I hope you can understand my delicate position here, Peggy. While I would love to bring her to you, the neighbors...you know."

Peggy nodded. "*Oui*, I understand. Did she...Is she...?" "*Bon*. All is well, then," he said standing, looking at his watch, and heading to the door." Oh, *Monsieur Berceuse*," she stopped him as he left the bungalow. "*Oui*, Yellow bird." "When will I go home? I want to see..." Henri hesitated. "It is better this way, yellow bird. This way, everybody is happy. Oh, by the way, try to call me Henri sometimes, *d'accord*?"

Yolette became a frequent visitor to the bungalow, then. Gerard, the caretaker told Peggy that she came freely when Peggy was not home also. He didn't offer any further information, but she saw him shaking his head. She almost asked him why he was shaking his head, but she decided not to. Yolette always came with news of home. Peggy could ask her questions that she didn't dare ask Henri about the family. Yolette also had a man who wanted to marry her and she would amuse Peggy with stories of their affair.

Months passed, then years.

Haiti underwent numerous political changes. Yolette told her that the people had established Papa Doc Duvalier as president for life. They had had enough of the mulattos and Papa Doc had promised them liberty, equality, and fraternity, echoing the themes of the French Revolution many years prior. While many didn't know the meaning of those words, they understood this as their being free to wield their machetes without restraint and they did.

There followed a holocaust in which many mulattos were slaughtered in their own homes and their genitals severed, lit and wielded as cigars in the mouths of peasants drunk with *kleren* and with power.

Henri's brother, Carlos, had been burned alive in the palace courtyard as an example to all blacks who would not support Duvalier. Peggy worried because Henri had not been to the bungalow in a number of months and, as she told Yolette, she never knew how to contact him.

Then, she heard, again through Yolette, that Henri had gone to the American embassy and obtained political asylum and was living in the United States. She had never known while living in the small bungalow that he'd rented for her in *Petit Gouave* that he was an important man in the government. She felt lucky that she knew his first name! She only knew that she lived too far from anyone she knew. She often wondered how it was that Yolette could go back and forth from *Petit Gouave* to *Fort National* and she could not. What money Henri would give to her, he gave her with explicit instructions of what she should purchase with it. He was never mean, and he was sometimes tender; but always there was a clear if unspoken boundary which she dared not cross.

Peggy had become pregnant shortly after moving to Petit Gouave and had given birth to a baby girl and named her Kasha. She had foolishly hoped that Henri would have married her, somehow, but he did not because he was in exile. "Peggy, what are you going to do now," Yolette said, one day, throwing herself on Peggy's bed. "Who is going to pay for you to go to school? What about Kasha's milk?" She leaned up on one elbow, demanding to know from Peggy answers to questions that she herself did not know. Henri had put all her siblings in school as promised and had also put her in a school where she was learning French and typing. She had also begun studying for her diploma in nursing at the same time. She was intelligent and without all the younger brothers and sisters to take care of and numerous other chores, she found that learning was actually fun. She relished in the praise of her female instructors, but took care to feign humility when addressed by the young male teachers. She knew that being good-looking was dangerous, and feared that being pretty and intelligent might end in more trouble than she could manage. "Well, I am a good student. I can teach younger children at the school, I think. I have to finish my nursing studies. I like it. Kasha is doing okay with Carline watching her. I can...I don't know what to do, Yolette!" "*Bon*! I knew that. You know your friend won't let you drown in misery. I know a man named Antoine. He is a tailor. He is a mulatto...a *blan mannan*...a poor white man, but he works hard. He is handsome, but a little *sauvage*. As long as you don't make him jealous. He almost killed me once when...Anyway, I'll bring him here tomorrow and you can get to know him, *dako*? *Male!"*

And before Peggy could protest, Yolette was gone. She listened as her friend flirted shamelessly with the yard man, laughing as the man's wife cursed at him within everyone's earshot.

Antoine Ducasse was tall and husky, and rough, in sharp contrast to Henri's gentleness. Peggy feared his temper even worse than she feared the stuttering which preceded his frequent threats and punches.

At six foot, two inches, Antoine Ducasse was over two hundred and eighty pounds of unpredictable anger. His punishment was worse than Pepe's had ever been because he also cursed at her and called her names. Although he was the first man to ever tell her that he loved her, Peggy learned to cringe whenever he said that. He was extremely jealous and although he was married with four children, he imagined that she entertained numerous men whenever he was gone home.

This was a secret she could share with no one. Who could do anything anyway? He was a man and she was his woman. No one would interfere. If she had told, who would have intervened? Besides, Antoine had hinted numerous times that he dabbled in voodoo and had caused harm to countless and unnamed enemies. Peggy feared that he had trapped her in a web of voodoo and she didn't want to endanger anyone else by saying that out loud. Yolette had stopped coming around and Peggy wondered to herself if her friend had meant to help her by introducing her to Antoine...or if she had been a repository for the trash that she had found Antoine to be.

Still, she couldn't understand why Kasha didn't seem to like Antoine. He was good to the baby. He never even raised his voice at her, but often spoke to her in soft whispers, glancing over his shoulders at Peggy through narrowed eyes.

Still, Kasha screamed each time he picked her up and cried for Peggy to take her home to Mimi, who she called *Manman*. Peggy would have gladly obliged her except that Antoine complained that it was too long a trip from *Petit Gouave* to *Sans Fil* where Mimi now lived. It would cost too much money to put gas in his dilapidated Plymouth if he jumped each time Kasha decided to whine.

Many nights, after Peggy had settled down for the evening, Kasha would awaken in screams when Antoine only wanted to kiss the child good-night. It was embarrassing. Antoine said that he treated her like he treated exactly like his own four children, but the little brat never seemed to appreciate that at Peggy's house she could have apples and candies. She seemed to prefer the times when she stayed with Mimi in *Sans Fil*, dragging her butt through the filthy dust and playing with goat turds as if they were gold nuggets.

Kasha couldn't remember one time in her young life that she hadn't been anxious. As early as her first year, when Antoine would rub her back and kiss her good-night she had disliked him. If she cried, Peggy would smack her on the thigh and say harsh words that scared and quieted her. But she minded those less than Antoine's kisses that lasted too long on her lips and covered her nose making it hard for her to breathe.

Now, at age four, as she sat under a tree in the approaching darkness, Peggy was telling her that she could afford travel to the United States. She would be sending for Kasha as soon as she could work and make the money.

Henri's flirtation with politics and his subsequent exile had ended all hopes for the

Pouchot children to continue their education. It was now up to Peggy to find a new way.

Kasha swallowed and tears filled her eyes. She blinked hard, peering at the surrounding darkness, fearing that if her eyes filled with too much water, she would miss unknown and unspeakable horrors hidden by or approaching from the viscous darkness. "Don't cry, you little *macaque*. I will send you lots of new bows, panties, money and baby dolls."

Kasha struggled against her hug, and sniffed, "Will I be staying with my *manman*?" "*I* am your manman. I hope Mimi hasn't been telling you stories about how she fed you from her own breasts again," Peggy admonished, brows furrowing. "That was only because I had to work and go to school and Nani was still nursing when you were born. Besides, Yolette told me I would stay younger if I didn't let a child suck the life out of my breasts."

Peggy arched her back, sitting proudly, braless in the hot tropical night. "I *am* your manman," she repeated. "And you'll be taking Antoine with you," Kasha ventured. "Oh, so that's it. You'll be missing Antoine! No, he'll be with you for a couple of years until I can send for him." Kasha sobbed and strangled on tears and phlegm. She coughed spasmodically, her tiny frame trembling.

Peggy looked at her daughter's downcast eyes. "There's no pleasing you, is there, little monkey? There's no understanding you either."

A fleeting panic threatened to break through to Peggy and unbidden concern rooted in her heart cautioned a caveat as she scrutinized the little girl and realized that Kasha, like Antoine, had a habit of stuttering. Strange, since Kasha was, of course, Henri's child. She looked at the tiny pants that Kasha wore and reminded herself that Antoine truly liked the child. After all, he was always taking her to his shop to be measured for one outfit or another.

Peggy remembered that she herself never had more than one or two hand-me-down dresses at one time before the age of sixteen, and she inhaled resolutely, pursing her lips.

She shivered, looking around her. "Come inside, Kasha. It's getting dark, and the *lougarous* will be looking for little girls to eat tonight."

Peggy laughed as Kasha virtually flew past her skirt and made it inside even before she had finished speaking.

After Peggy left for the United States, Mimi seemed less inclined to pamper Kasha. It was almost as if there had been a competition for Kasha's affection and the nomenclature of *Manman* while Peggy was around. Without the two different people to run back and forth to, Kasha felt a sense of isolation that she had never known. She made her way precariously around the now lifeless house in *Sans Fils*, a ghetto just one step aboard Mimi's previous home in *Fort National*. Still, Peggy's small bungalow had been constructed of brick and cement and could withstand the deadly cyclones which so frequently and arbitrarily assailed the tiny island. Kasha would literally watch as fragile structures of sticks and mud float past her own sturdy edifice. Now, again, she lived a life of constant danger and fear. Growing up in Mimi's house, she was constantly reminded that she did not belong, especially by Nani and Nisia, who were closest in age to her.

Those two, the youngest of Mimi's daughters, were jealous of what they perceived to be some sort of extreme pampering that Kasha was receiving from Mimi. To them, the fact that Peggy was sending one hundred American dollars per month for Kasha's care should not have meant that Kasha would receive a drumstick versus a chicken foot with her cornmeal and black beans. Then, of course, the daily half-liter of unpasteurized sun-temperature milk that was contracted from a filthy merchant for Kasha's consumption was to be coveted. So what if by the time it was boiled over the coals to kill whatever microbes might be festering in it, the final outcome was only a half cup of thick white substance with a layer of probably germ-filled scum called "cream" on top. All this was perceived as special treatment.

So, every once in a while, one of her many aunts and uncles would walk by, and for the sheer pleasure of it, give her a *zoklo*, or a clunk on the head with their knuckles.

Kasha could not understand why she was seen as special, but they were always telling her she was treated specially and so she despised being special. Being special made her the target of derision or pain or loss. The constant fear made her feel tired and alone. Her dark and limpid eyes always appeared swollen, as if she had not slept.

Still, Kasha's life had been virtually manageable after Antoine's departure to join Peggy in New York. She'd only had to protect her friendship with Judith. That hadn't been too hard. Naturally, the treatment she received from her mother's youngest siblings made her seek out the neighbor girl, Judith, even more.

Kasha had grown accustomed to the scorn which she had to endure because she enjoyed spending time with Judith so much. Kasha could not play openly with Judith. Judith was considered filthy and she often was. Judith's family might have been one rung below the poverty ladder as compared to Kasha's own family. Her stepfather was a *gendarme*.

Judith was thick and ugly and seemed to thrive in the dark and busy corridor that ran parallel to the Pouchot house. She was there day or night and seemed to fear nothing. She also perceived Kasha as special by virtue of the fact that Kasha had kin abroad.

Kasha also had the luxury of going to school, and Judith's stepfather's salary as a *gendarme* could not provide an education for the young girl.

Meanwhile, Kasha was sent to a private school, the *Ecole Mixte du Sacre Coeur*. The Coed school of the Sacred Heart was a frightening place for Kasha, but Judith did not want to hear it. She preferred to discuss how Kasha's family must be rich because her own family rented one of four narrow, dark, wooden bungalows from Mimi and Pepe.

Judith would whine, "*You* live in a house made of cement. *Your* house is painted. *Your* house has those nice designs cut into the cement that let you see outside without leaving the house. *Your* house is painted pink and blue, colors that show in the sky when the sun is going down. *And*, at *Mardi Gras* time, all the neighbors go on *your* roof to watch the parades go by without being pushed by the crowds, and the roof never even falls in!"

Kasha thought that Judith made that last statement with a note of regret in her voice.

Judith would continue, "Those of us living in the apartments have to use the *back* latrine, the filthy and disgusting one that every renter has to use and that you're not even *allowed* to use."

Kasha wanted to say so much, but the fierce look on Judith's black moon face and the sweaty beads on her forehead when she got in that mood choked back Kasha's thoughts and kept them imprisoned in her throat.

She wanted to tell Judith how she hated *Mardi Gras* parades because just looking down at the participants in the February festival terrified her. Their costumes were either very beautiful or very terrifying and fear provoking. Many of the revelers were crazed by the hot sun and cheap *kleren* and would bump into each other and often trample each other underfoot. Too often, fights would break out between the observers and the participants. Kasha, watching from the roof would feel woozy. The constant whistle blowing and loud *Rara* music was often deafening. She never rushed to the roof to watch. She always had to be dragged to the roof by Judith.

She wanted to tell Judith that she found the Pouchot's own private latrine just as disgusting as the neighbors'. She wanted to tell her of various, mysterious stains on the concrete wall of the tiny enclosed latrine. In the darkness and heat of the unlit latrine, she had been at once curious and disgusted at the substance evacuating her body and would play a game of listening for the plop that would come moments later as it reached the bottom some thirty feet below. Once, she had touched her feces as it exited her body, felt it, marveling. She had smashed it in her fingers, at once fascinated and repulsed. She had brought it up to her nose, smelled it, and stuck her tongue out and actually attempted to taste it. Someone calling to another person outside the door had caused her to hurriedly and shamefully smear it against the wall instead.

There was no running water in the house at *Sans Fil*. That precious substance, sources unknown, had to be purchased from women passing by with buckets full on their heads. There had been no one, therefore, to stand over her and ask her questions such as, "Did you wash your hands with soap and water, making sure you cleaned between the fingers and under the fingernails?"

Later that day, as she walked past Nani with her head lowered so as not to provoke any tongue lashing, the older girl had only sneered, "Humph. You're even beginning to smell like that Judith girl. You're getting as black and pimply as she is from playing with her out under the hot sun. Soon, you are going to look like her."

Nani had walked away, giggling, swinging her now ample behind, aware of the hurt she had caused the sensitive Kasha and enjoying it.

Kasha had wondered quietly and with amazement why Nani didn't notice that she was at *least* as black-skinned as the neighbor girl she so loved to criticize.

She longed to share with her friend stories about the close encounter she had with the bottom of the latrine one time. That was when a terrific bout of tropical prickly heat overwhelmed her one hot August afternoon as she attempted to move her bowels.

She had been so scared as she remembered that someone had left the latrine door open some time before and a curious goat kid had wandered in and drowned in the excrement. Judith had spent the entire time laughing at the plight of the goat. Kasha had spent her time, heart beating like so many voodoo drums, praying that the men who were brought in from the neighborhood with various ladders would be able to rescue the poor goat. That had been one time that she had kept her ears open for the sound of suffering, as busy men briskly brushed her aside. At last, the poor animal had stopped bleating. It had stopped struggling. Kasha remembered breathing out, finally. She felt so much like that struggling, kicking kid sometimes. She just was not allowed to cry out because everyone would tell her how lucky she was and how ashamed she should feel.

Pepe had sworn profusely and Kasha and Judith had scurried away before they could become the object of his rage. He had still had to pay the men for trying to crawl down the slimy walls inside the latrine itself. The animal could not be recovered to be slaughtered. There was no meat to be sold to unsuspecting buyers.

Still, the Pouchots were considered special by those around them because they at least cooked and ate once a day. Mimi was a *missionary dame* at the local evangelical church of the apostolic faith, whatever that meant. As such, she entertained many people from church and from abroad. Her home was even used once to house a visiting white missionary passing through Port-au-Prince on her way to some rural area. She had been a sight to the Pouchots and a curiosity to the neighbors. The white woman may have weighed just over 150 pounds, but to the thin and wiry people around her, she seemed immense and they associated that with wealth and luxury.

Kasha had asked Mimi why the woman was so big and had been answered the following way: "All white people are that big. The Bible says that when God sent His son, Jesus, to the earth. He sent Him first to Indian people who lived in Haiti at that time. They were called Arawaks. They didn't receive His message, so He rejected them and punished them so that almost all of them have disappeared from the world. Actually, white people who welcomed Jesus years later would come to wipe out the Indians from the face of Haiti."

Kasha looked suspiciously at Mimi. What she was saying about Jesus seemed familiar enough. She had heard of Him in church. She wondered if Mimi was just answering any old thing just to get rid of her. She tried again. "What about us black Haitian people, what did we do wrong for us to suffer so much?" Kasha asked curiously. She was eager to right the wrong and make things right for everyone. She never imagined black people outside of Haiti. All foreigners *had* to be white. "Well," Mimi continued hurriedly, and she seemed annoyed as she attempted to season the pork for dinner and to answer Kasha's multitude of questions at the same time. "When Jesus came to black people, they were in a place called *Afrique*. They were rich and they were smart and they had

69

many animals and many feasts. The men had many wives and the women had many children and they all ate and slept. They had all they wanted." "Black people were many and of different shades of color. They spoke the same language. But they did not welcome Jesus, either. They practiced idolatry and worshipped the trees and their dead grandmothers and grandfathers, instead of God. So, He punished them and changed all their languages so that they wouldn't speak with each other anymore and they had to move away from each other. Because there were many different groups now, the children ran wild and the groups went to war and brothers killed brothers and fathers killed sons and they never even knew it. They couldn't recognize each other."

Mimi continued, "That happened in a place called *Babel* in *Afrique* and that is why black people have suffered so much." "The African brothers were sometimes treacherous and so they sold each other to white people for fancy blankets and weapons and other things God had ever meant for them to have. Many years later, I learned in school (Mind you, I only went for two years, but I listened and I learned)...I learned that God had sent white people to *Afrique* to bring many of these people to Haiti because all the Indians had been killed. God still loved Haiti and blessed it with gold and water and trees, but He hated those people who had rejected His Son. So, He is still punishing us today." "Mimi, why doesn't God just kill us like He did with people on the Earth when He told Noah to build the boat? Wouldn't that be nicer than letting us suffer?"

Mimi stopped pounding the mixture of garlic, parsley, thyme and salt for the seasoning and looked quizzically but harshly at Kasha. Kasha drew back instantly, expecting a rebuke. "Us suffer? *You* have never known suffering, Kasha. You are lucky. In this house, we eat two times a day. We sleep under a roof. We have shelter. We have water to drink! Ha! Be careful what you say, child! God does not like people who are ungrateful. He is God, the *Bon Die*. He does what He will and He has reasons for everything He does. We must never question His will! Do you understand?" "*Oui*," Kasha answered, sheepishly. She silently wished God would ignore her and not bother with her. It was too confusing what to do to please Him. Now, people couldn't even question Him!

Kasha waited until Mimi had resumed pounding the spices to the pulp that would make the meat so delicious. "So, white people received God's son as guests into their houses? Is that why they're so big and rich? Is that why they can come to Haiti and visit and live and own shops and have maids? Is that why the mulattos have so much too, because they are so close to being white that some of them even look white?" "Yes, yes, Kasha. *Padon, padon*, out of the way. When will you be old enough to help instead of asking so many questions? When your mother, Peggy was your age, she could scrub a pot clean and then cook a meal fit for a king in it! I think I spoil you too much. Peggy was right. Now, go play!"

Kasha ran out of the small outdoor and windowless kitchen, the pleasant and familiar smell of burning charcoal and spices still in her nostrils. She ran to find Judith to tell her what she had learned from Mimi.

Judith listened intently as Kasha described the nameless missionary and all the special things that were being done for her to make her welcome. "Mimi says that she might be an angel in disguise. Mimi said that in the Bible, a man named Abraham once welcomed and cooked for angels and God blessed his old wife with a baby."

Judith demanded with a harsh barking laugh, "Why would Mimi want a baby? She already has thirteen children and you! Maybe she wants a dog since she killed your puppy with that big piece of wood last month." Judith paused to allow the memory to sink in for Kasha for full effect.

"Remember?" Judith whispered insistently. "Remember, when Altagrace, the neighbor got into the argument with Mimi and your little puppy Prince started barking and Altagrace accused your *grann*, Mimi, of sending a demon to possess the puppy to answer her and your *grann* got mad and beat your puppy into peanut butter?"

Judith stopped talking again, realizing that she had been talking real fast and relishing the fact that all of Kasha's excitement about having a white missionary in her house, and all of her stupid stories about *Afrique* and the Bible had faded from her eyes.

Judith wondered why she was so mean to Kasha. She enjoyed the stories and she wanted to hear more, but she continued, despite herself. "Anyway, a lady that big probably eats a lot, so *I'm* glad that she's not at *my* house." "I know," Kasha agreed readily. "You're lucky. I'm sure she's not an angel anyway. She hasn't done any miracle or anything. She just sits in that room and eats. I had to take out all the sleeping rags and sweep the dirt floor and work so hard before she got here. She hasn't even touched me or offered me a *benediction* like the missionaries do at church. I bring her in fresh mangoes and pineapples. Mimi sends in rice, chicken, legumes. She eats it all and then waits for us to come get the dirty dishes and cups. This morning, when I brought her the red and white vase that we girls in the house all use to wash our bottom, she peed in it right in front of me. I ran out, wondering if she was going to wash her private in the pee water in front of me too. Wait till you hear this. She came out for the first time, as she handed me the vase. She was smiling for the first time too. She had made caca in it! Judith, white people's caca smells bad too!"

The tension was gone for the moment. The girls rolled on the concrete roof laughing, holding their stomachs. For one brief moment, there was a genuine warmth between the two girls.

Deep inside, Kasha was disappointed. She had not imagined that white missionaries could do such disgusting things as move their bowels. She made up her mind that there was no possibility of the woman being an angel, and Kasha endeavored to stay away from her rather than volunteering to take things into the room to her. There would be no blessings forthcoming. Kasha never even knew when the woman left.

When Kasha was eight years old, she finally met Peggy again. Peggy had come in from New York at three o'clock one morning. She was fat and even yellower than Kasha remembered. She had become loud and laughed a lot and mixed in a lot of words that no one understood that Kasha imagined was English. When Peggy laughed, everyone around her laughed. Kasha felt this had to do with four large and bulky looking suitcases which she had brought with her. Kasha longed for her to stay because everyone seemed happy with everyone else because Peggy was back with presents and laughter and stories from the United States. She thought that if Peggy stayed, everything would magically be better. She evaded Antoine, who stared at her in a way that she seemed to recognize or remember. She only knew that the look made her uneasy, and he kept reaching for her shoulders and squeezing them too hard and telling her what a big girl she had become while scrutinizing her through eyes that were fathomless slits. After a week of gleefully handing out handfuls of pennies to neighborhood children who had begun to haunt the Pouchot residence like scavengers around a carcass, Peggy left in the middle of the night without saying good-bye to Kasha.

Just like that.

Kasha searched her mind for a reference in the adult conversations which she was not permitted to hear that might have been an intimation of when Peggy was leaving. It was as if she had never even been there. Things went back to normal. Kasha felt dejected and morose.

Kasha went back to seeking out Judith, whom she had not seen in the week that Peggy was in town.

At first, Judith ignored her and called her names like "show-off" and said hurtful things like, "You don't even look like her. She's yellow and fat and pretty. *You're* black and scrawny and ugly."

Kasha ignored those comments and tried to turn Judith's anger toward her into sympathy. She told Judith that of all the pretty things that Peggy had brought, she was not allowed to wear any of them! Mimi said they were to be saved for special occasions because Kasha would just drag her butt in the dirt with Judith and destroy them anyway. Still, Nani got to wear some of them to school. Kasha promised Judith that she would steal some of the pretty "jersey" underwear for Judith, but in her heart, she doubted that they would fit Judith's big derriere.

Like many things that Mimi packed away for special occasions, Kasha never saw those new pairs of panties again.

Kasha and Judith continued their strange friendship, digging deep in the dirt for snail shells and pieces of broken pottery that they pretended were money. Some of the broken pieces of pottery were shiny and very ornate with strange golden designs. They wondered who might have owned dishes like that when their own were made out of aluminum. They threw them out when they were done playing. They continued to eat mangoes and to use the seeds as doll babies, talking to them, chiding them, braiding the stringy mango "hair". As good mothers, they spanked their mango babies also, speaking harshly to them, just as they were spoken to by their caregivers.

One sultry Haitian afternoon, Judith and Kasha bustled covertly from the Pouchot latrine to a small apartment up what remained of once concrete steps. The two friends ran up and down the half cement and half dust stumps, giggling from unspeakable excitement and fear.

They were looking for Maricienne, an eleven year old *restavek* who worked hard for her food and lodging while other children played. Maricienne's origins and kin were unknown. She had been brought in by Rosette's husband, one of the tenants, and introduced as a niece from La Tortue. Things had deteriorated between Rosette and her husband, Dieuvil, from that point on. They argued loudly and frequently and every once in a while to end the arguments, Rosette would be beaten by Dieuvil. Rosette would run into the yard screaming for help in view of the entire *lakou* . Some laughed, mostly the men and children. The women would sigh, and blame Rosette for talking back to her husband and causing problems in the yard. "After all," they would say loudly amid Rosette's howls of pain, "A woman should know better than to talk back to her husband." They had learned that important lesson, themselves.

So, the cycle continued: Dieuvil beat Rosette, Rosette beat Maricienne. The women in the *Lakou* speculated that in that one room flat, Dieuvil probably copulated with the pre-pubescent and malnourished Maricienne in plain view of Rosette just to spite her. At least, that's what Judith told Kasha that she'd heard from her stepfather and mother.

Kasha would never get a chance to hear such juicy tidbits. She knew to make herself scarce when adults started whispering. There must have been different rules in Judith's house.

That afternoon, there were no adults around for some strange reason. It was not a school day, and had it been, Judith would not have been in school anyway. Her stepfather had made a weak attempt to send her to school at the mother's constant pleading. But, the uniforms, monthly tuition, personal chalkboard and other accouterments proved too expensive. After two months, Judith had suddenly stopped attending the public school which she had walked so far to reach every day. The rumor was quietly and quickly spread through the neighborhood grapevine that voodoo was at the root of this new misfortune. Judith told it to Kasha this way: "Kasha, whenever I sat in class, the teachers spoke in French. I don't know French. They are Haitian too. Why don't they speak to me in *Kreyol*? One of the schoolmasters looks just like my uncle Michel, but he is the meanest. He beats me every day with a big stick that has many thick pieces of red animal skin hanging from it. It's like a stick with many belts attached to it. It looks like a giant red spider. Just because I can't understand when he yells at me in French to get to the board and write." Judith twisted her lips and sucked her teeth. "How am I supposed to write? That's why I go to school; 'cause I don't know how. Anyway, one day, when I was on my way to school, I began to see big stars of light and then blackness, light and then blackness over and over and over again. When I finally got to school and sat in my seat, I heard a lot of noise and everything looked black."

Judith spoke faster, as she did when she became excited or angry. She seemed to be reliving the panic and shame she had experienced at school. Her eyes squinted to an almost close as she looked painfully back. "I felt like that fat black goat must have felt at Veyo the witchdoctor's ceremony last year. You remember! You and me snuck up when we heard the drums and chanting. Kasha? Remember what we heard? Drums and shouting and laughing. Remember when we peeped through the rot in the gate? Remember what we saw, Kasha? Men shaking their hips and waving machetes, women chanting ancient songs and calling for the *louas* and spirits to possess them; and that poor goat in the middle, all the while trying to find a crack to escape."

Kasha wanted Judith to stop talking. The frightening memory threatened to drag her physically back to suck her through the holes in the gate through which they had frightfully peeked at the madness. But Judith had to continue. "Kasha, look at me! I'm talking to you! Anyway, I felt like that big fat black goat that day in school. Everyone was reciting in French. My hands were sweating and leaving wet marks on the black chalkboard where he had sent me to write while everyone recited. Because the board was wet, the chalk was not writing on it anymore . Even still, everybody else recited, chanting the words like the women at the voodoo ceremony. He sent me back to my desk to write on the paper."

Judith continued, "He kept cracking on my knuckles with a ruler each time I tried and did it wrong. I was crying and my tears were falling on the paper so that I couldn't see anything I was trying to do, but I kept putting the pencil to the paper because I knew I would keep doing it wrong. Then, he would keep hitting me and I would keep making mistakes and I knew there would come a time when he would get tired of hitting me and start some other activity with the other children. Kasha, I erased until I made a big hole in that paper. Then, he brought out that big *rigoise*. It's about sixty pieces of vine that they wet and twist and let dry, and wet and twist new pieces onto it and braid it together until it's thicker than a palmist branch. It doesn't even bend when they beat you with that! The last thing I heard was him calling me a *roach*!"

Kasha shook her head slowly. She wanted to say that she had seen a boy get the *rigoise* treatment once for not knowing his lesson. From then on, she had made sure she always memorized those chapters in French even if she often had no idea what most of the words meant. But, she was scared silent by the look in Judith's eyes. Judith was not looking at her. Judith didn't want an answer. She just wanted to talk. "After that day, each time I walked the road to school, I would hear the voodoo drums from Veyo's yard and see that goat running around in circles with all the noise around him and what they finally did to him. Remember? They took that machete, and while that goat was still running..." "*Ase!* Stop!" Kasha jumped up and ran up the steps, while Judith mercilessly followed." *Kapon* ! Chicken," Judith called after her.

Still, Judith was back from that trance now, laughing at her, seeming to be in derision, dancing around her, calling her skinny chicken and displaying her gleaming white teeth below beautiful purplish-black gums. "Anyway, you know what? When I told my stepfather, he went to a *boko* and they told him some jealous neighbor who didn't have the money to send their kid to school had fixed me so I could never learn. He said it didn't make sense to try to fight voodoo magic. He said I couldn't go to school anymore. I don't care. I never liked it anyway."

Kasha brought the conversation back to the present. "Where's Maricienne, and why have we been running up and down these steps looking for her? *Aiieeee!* See? A rock cut my foot and I'm bleeding now," she whined. She lifted a foot to show Judith, but the girl was intent on finding Maricienne now that she had succeeded in scaring the wits out of Kasha with her stories of voodoo, goats and school. "I don't know where she is. She said that her and Kenol were going to do the *ti bagay*, the little thing. *You* know." "What little thing?" Kasha whispered since Judith had lowered her own voice. "*Egare*! Stupid," exclaimed the more worldly Judith. They are going to do *it*!

"What!" hissed Kasha, warily. "Shhhh!"

They had returned to the common latrine and they could hear furtive noises from the fourteen-year-old Kenol and the eleven-year-old wretch. You stay here and watch to make sure no grown-up comes to use the latrine. I told them I would come in and watch and they were going to teach me how to do it, too. When I'm done, you come in, and I'll keep watch, okay?"

Kasha looked around, wild-eyed, terrified of being discovered and started to protest, but nine-year-old Judith had already crammed herself in the latrine with the other two. Kasha imagined what would happen if Mimi caught her lurking around the neighbors' stinking latrine, looking as nervous as she felt. Mimi would immediately know that something was up, and she would be the one to get a spanking. And what if someone needed to use the latrine? What was she to tell them? Judith hadn't told her that part!

She put her ear to the door of the latrine, listening, feeling a strange titillation. There was a lot of talking and protesting and giggling all at once. She sensed a strange excitement and nervousness and wanted to fling open the door and see what *it* was they were doing in there. Whatever *it* was sounded dangerous, but fun. It was the dangerous part she did not like. The common latrine was small. What if one of them fell in?

From inside the house, she heard Nani call out to someone. Kasha bolted! She wasn't sure where to run so she ran through the corridor and came in panting through the front door of the house to run right into Nani. "Where have you been and why are you sweating like a butchered pig?" demanded Nani.

Kasha murmured, "I...I feel sick. My stomach hurts." "Humph! Maybe too much of that milk my manman is always spoiling you with! I can't wait for you to be sent to New York to your mother like they're saying." Still, Nani mercifully left the room, and Kasha threw herself down on the rags which covered the floor for her bedding that night. She lay there for a long time, wondering what Nani's last remark about her going to New York meant.

Some months later, Kasha stood shivering at John F. Kennedy Airport in New York City. She wondered sadly what Judith was doing at that moment.

Kasha had never known what it was to feel cold. It was October and a wet rain pounded through a scarce early snowfall.

The plane trip over to JFK airport had been frightening. To be so high up in the air with nothing but God holding you up!

Mimi, accompanying her, had retched unabashedly in one bag, while she held a bag under Kasha's mouth. Those seated around them glared contemptuously as they attempted to consume their food, served amid the incessant noise and smell of vomit.

When Kasha had expectantly popped what looked like a green grape into her dry mouth, it had a sour and bitter taste and the shock of it caused her to sputter and retch even more.

Some disembodied voice from somewhere on the plane mumbled, "You've never had an olive before, have you?" Then, "No, of course not. Poor little devil."

What kind of world was it where even a grape tasted bad?

Kasha stood in the street outside the airport, teeth chattering. Peggy wrapped a long, heavy coat around Mimi and they hurried through to Antoine's car. Kasha followed quickly, afraid she would be left behind and lost in the big airport in a strange country.

Peggy looked like a fat animal covered with fur, and was barely recognizable to her daughter. She spoke hurriedly, in English, Kasha guessed. When she tiptoed to offer the customary kiss of greeting, Kasha found that Peggy was bending to offer her own mother a kiss. She didn't attempt a second time.

Mimi had agreed to live with Antoine and Peggy in a spacious apartment in Brooklyn, but she could not stand the incessant battles that went on between the two. Worse yet, the cursing...the names that Antoine would call Peggy, not even respecting that Mimi was present in the room. When Peggy left the house to one of her many housecleaning jobs, the horrendous stories of strange sexual acts between Peggy and countless other persons, male or female were nauseating. Mimi did not believe the incredulous stories but Antoine seemed so convinced and could cite locations and names.

Either the man was a liar or a lunatic and Mimi could not worship her Jesus in that environment.

She worried for Kasha, who seemed to avoid Antoine at all costs, but children were strange. Had she not struggled to raise her own brood like a mother hen without Pepe's help? Kasha seemed civil and polite and Peggy said she was doing well in school and learning English. She was a smart little girl, always had been. Well, she would do for Kasha as she had done for her own children. She would yield her to God's mercy and grace and trust that she would be safe.

Mimi fought to not believe Antoine's stories, but she began to not look at Peggy again. Peggy would come home tired and tense. She was nasty to everyone around her as she wondered why everyone avoided contact with her. Hadn't she worked hard to send for them all, Antoine included? But now, there was always tension in her house. They all treated her like she was a lougarou who had consumed their firstborn! Finally, Mimi could take no more. She moved in with Regine in Manhattan and watched Regine's children while she went out in the snow to clean hotels and make beds.

When Mimi left and went to Manhattan, Antoine began telling the stories to Kasha. Kasha always felt uncomfortable and sick to her stomach and wanted to tell him to stop, but that would be rude. He was an adult and whatever he said or did was right.

She thought she had it all figured out one day when she told him that she didn't understand what he was saying, but he seemed to look happy about that. He had stopped talking, but later on, he brought home many books filled with pictures of people doing terrible things to each other's private parts and yelled at Kasha if she refused to look. Kasha tried hard to direct her eye to the pictures while forcing her eyes not to focus. The result was a blur of madness to her eyes and mind.

Kasha got an idea. She approached Antoine tentatively one day and asked if they could show the pictures to Peggy. Antoine responded that Peggy was jealous of her and would not let him show her those pictures because they would make Kasha prettier as well as smarter than her mother. Kasha did not believe this, but her mind was no match for Antoine's in cunning.

Another time, she told Antoine that she did not like the pictures. She was tired of them, but thanked him anyway for teaching her so much. She had dared to ask, "Who's teaching your daughter in Haiti those very important things that you say I need to learn?" Antoine had paused before answering, "I taught her enough myself before I left Haiti," and Kasha had found herself feeling sorry for a girl she had never even seen. When she had asked, "Well, why do I need to know this stuff anyway," he had used her recent involvement with a church youth group to answer. "Don't they read that Bible to you in that church? It is supposed to be the Word of God to you and it tells us to multiply and fill the earth."

Kasha had persisted, "But I know my arithmetic very well. I ranked second in my class last year!"

Antoine, who always seemed to find something funny when Kasha was feeling her most desperate and helpless, had laughed so hard that she had expected a gush of stinking bilious pee to flow from the disgusting thing he manipulated in his hand as he gave her this "Bible" lesson. "No, little monkey. Multiplying in the Bible has nothing to do with how smart you are. Any beast can multiply the way God wants it done. You just lay down together and have babies. That's what I have been trying to teach you. To do God's will like you pretend you want to. But you are stubborn and you are disobedient to me and you are also disobedient to God, who wants you to honor your parents! You'll probably burn in hell if you don't do as I say."

All Kasha could manage in response to this was a muttering under her breath. "I'm not a beast," she told herself, repeatedly.

Kasha was in a dilemma. She didn't want to lie down with anybody. It always made her feel so small and as if she couldn't do anything for herself.

She didn't want babies.

She didn't want to burn in hell, either, and she didn't want to go to heaven where Antoine was obviously going because he seemed to be so obedient to God.

He had continued with some story of how a young girl had done her job in teaching him when he had been just four years old:

She had been one of the many motherless restavek in Haiti. An aunt had sent her to Antoine's mother when she was just ten years old. Supposedly, the aunt's husband could not tolerate the girl, for reasons unknown. In exchange for scraps of food and a roof over her head, Saintilia would care for Antoine, kill chickens for dinner, as necessary, and keep the house clean. Her caring for Antoine included bathing him.

Lacking the accouterments of childhood, she toyed with him as a child of means would toy with a doll with many intricate parts. The young Antoine did not understand why the games had to be played in secret. Saintilia was kind and good to him and gave equal attention to the shiny curly hair on his head as she gave to other, more hidden parts. Saintilia taught him many dark secrets she had learned from her boko uncle as she sang words that had their origin in the ancient Congo. She sang of Damballah Weydo, the snake god and of Sanntayigwe, the vengeful.

Antoine was always filled with a dark excitement when she would decide to play with him. He was always guaranteed an exciting and scary story to keep him distracted.

Antoine had watched the many changes in Saintilia's body over the five-year period that she lived with him. At fifteen, she was a marvel to look at. After a while though, she began to not be so readily available to him.

He was angry. He had always played when she wanted! He had spied her sneaking around the back of the outhouse with Arnold, a boy who worked as a restavek to the neighbors.

Arnold was a big boy, not like Antoine. Antoine became angrier and angrier until one day he told his mother about Saintilia and Arnold just after they had been behind the latrine for a little while. He had expected that Saintilia would be beaten with the belt as she had been numerous times before when Antoine had tattled on her about some other things. Instead, she had been ridiculed in front of all the neighbors and had been discharged in shame.

Before she had left, Saintilia found Antoine sulking in his room. She looked at him with red eyes and spat, "You disgusting little vagabond! You're just jealous! I don't know where I'm going to live except for the streets. You'll pay for this! Now, you can fuck the chickens and pull on the goats' tits!"

And Antoine did just that. He would immobilize the poor birds by twisting their necks until they were almost suffocated and would then force himself into them. He never did bother the goats, however. He was afraid of them.

Kasha watched Antoine's eyes narrow as he relived the stories he told of his childhood and thought that if there was a devil, he lived with her.

Kasha began to hate herself. She had tried so many ways to make Antoine stop the stories and the touching and the pictures. She had failed. She began to dress like a boy. She despised the breasts that insisted on sprouting on her chest. She slept on her stomach so that she could flatten them. She wore brassieres that were too small so as to appear smaller-breasted.

Antoine seemed fascinated by her physical changes. He asked her strange questions. "Did you find anything wet in your panties today?"

Kasha was indignant. She had not wet the bed since she was five years old! He must really find her stupid!

Then, her dirty panties began to disappear. He told her that he was keeping them to make strong magic so she would love him. She didn't want to love him, but she feared him too much to tell him that.

She felt constantly dirty, although she would bathe every time she got a chance. She felt as if some invisible signal was coming from her body that everyone but her could see.

She refused to undress for gym class at school for fear the other girls would recognize the changes that she was certain Antoine was causing in her. She wore her gym uniform under her clothes and the other girls laughed at her. She laughed with them outwardly when one of them suggested that Kasha might be missing a piece of something. She wondered if, in fact, there were not some hidden evil in her seventy-five pound frame.

At home, the accusations toward Peggy continued and Antoine promised to kill her with his long, sharp tailor scissors and make Kasha watch if Kasha revealed their secret activities. Kasha believed him. She would watch him beat Peggy many times and once, he had come close to killing her. Afterward, Peggy would take Kasha on long subway rides to far away places. They would find a bench in some station and cry next to each other, even if not together. Kasha liked those times. Eventually, Peggy would rise, and they would silently return to Antoine's apartment.

Still, everything would stop for a while. And then, just when Kasha thought it was all over, there would be another terrible fight between Antoine and Peggy. Kasha thought it was much like the coming of the cyclones in Haiti.

Kasha was awakened by the noise of it one night. Antoine was holding a large pair of tailor scissors over his head and Peggy was wielding a pot of boiling water. Kasha covered her head and counted in her mind the numbers on the calendars: "1-8-15-22-29; 2-9-16-23-30; 3-10-17-24-31; 4-11-18-25; 5-12-19-26; 6-13-20-27; 7-14-21-28; 1-8-15..."

Her heart pounded first in her throat and then in her ears like many voodoo drums.

She had counted over and over. Somehow, she either fainted or fell asleep.

The next day when they were alone, she had begged Antoine not to kill Peggy. "She's the only *manman* I have now that Mimi has moved away."

Antoine promised that he would not, laughing all the while. There was a new twist to the things he wanted to teach Kasha, though. If she didn't let him or if she told anyone, he would have to kill Peggy. He said that Kasha's disobedience would force him to.

Kasha was determined to keep the secrets, not because she loved Peggy, but because she feared what Peggy's death would mean. She would be alone with Antoine in Brooklyn. Everyone else lived in Manhattan and they all probably thought that Antoine absolutely spoiled her and that she was a brat for not returning his affection.

Many times, Kasha wanted to tell Mimi, but some unspeakable something warned her to stay quiet. Mimi would not believe her. Kasha would be punished. Everyone would yell at her. Somehow, it would be all her fault.

And so she counted, whenever Antoine would swing his heavy hairy leg over her slight and petite frame: "1-8-15-22-29; 2-9-16-23-30; 3-10...." She could not breathe with his weight on her. Her chest hurt... "17-23...or was it 24..."

And the years dragged on mercilessly.

When Kasha turned twelve, she dreamed of killing herself. She would hide under the bed in the Brooklyn apartment which she shared with Antoine, Peggy, and their two new children. Peggy was very busy working two or three jobs going to school and staying away from home. Kasha was conscientious and did the housework and took care of the younger kids when she got home from school. She sometimes wondered why the baby-sitter would look at her with such pity whenever she went next door to pick up the two younger children after school. She avoided the woman's gaze, fearing she knew about Antoine. Kasha felt responsible for what was going on with Antoine.

She felt sure that if Antoine were her *real* father, he wouldn't hurt her as he did.

No one ever knew that she would hide under the bed and they would call her "dirty" for doing it.

She did all she could to avoid contact with Antoine, whose touches and kisses had become a mundane, though odious part of her life. She never dared tell Peggy any of this. The understanding was that if she kept the secret and met Antoine at his tailor shop every morning before school, he wouldn't curse and scream and beat Peggy anymore. The yelling and cursing were what caused that pounding in her ears, so she worked hard to prevent it. Antoine didn't always keep his part of this bargain, but she feared also that he might begin to beat her, too; and so she treaded the narrow and precarious balance beam that was her life.

Antoine always offered her handfuls of quarters afterward, and she would always reject those, even if she were hungry. She would go and ask Peggy for fifty cents for lunch and she was always rewarded instead with a long story of how hard Peggy worked. Didn't she notice that there were now two other children in the house, and how could a child be so selfish? At the end of the speech, Kasha would gravely accept the two quarters that were thrust into her palm and then make it a point to return the money to Peggy's purse when the latter left the room. After a while, she stopped asking, but she also kept refusing Antoine's offers of money. Something she had learned in school about bad girls who let men touch them for money kept her from taking what she felt she deserved for putting up with his constant pestering. Yet, she helped herself to his cash register at his tailor shop in Brooklyn for months. She didn't know how to stop his actions, but she felt proud and strong inside that she could reject his offers of money.

Then one day, she realized that he was purposely stocking it with quarters. He had found her out. She resolved not to take anymore, as long as he meant for her to take it. It was only then that Antoine told Peggy that Kasha was taking his money from the store...after she had stopped doing so.

It was terrible. Kasha had to listen to, "How could you shame me like this?" And "My family has never had thieves in it before." Again, "Don't you know what they do to thieves in Haiti? They cut off their hands! Wait till I tell Mimi what her precious baby did! She'll never let you call her *manman* again! *I* am your mother. If you needed money, all you had to do was ask me."

Kasha remained quiet through all of this, crying silently and praying that she could die right then and there. It would never occur to her to interrupt while adults were speaking, regardless of what she had to say, and even if they were wrong. Kasha was mortified. She looked at Antoine for help, but he met her gaze and actually looked hurt. Kasha alone knew the real reason he was hurt.

She squinted her eyes and prayed hard, and when what she wished for didn't happen, she determined to find her real father.

Her real father would be good to her.

Peggy continued the barrage of words hurled at Kasha, and Kasha barely heard her.

Kasha missed Mimi. Mimi, who had raised Kasha to be a young lady, never laughing too loud, and never saying "*Non*" to her elders! Kasha would do just fine and would end up being a source of praise for Mimi, who kept a picture of Kasha in her Bible. Kasha took the subway to visit Mimi in Manhattan every Sunday after church. She wanted so much for Mimi to know that she was still a good girl. Mimi would listen. She never asked Kasha questions. She never heard more than Kasha had the courage to tell. She was never told more than Kasha knew would please her.

But, Mimi was gone.

Peggy could not or would not take Kasha's side.

After that scene with Peggy, Antoine avoided her at the house, but made sure that he always left early enough to wait for her on the road to school. At times, Kasha would take different routes, but by the time she neared school, Antoine would overtake her, and his catlike grin would indicate to her that he had won the game once again. For her part, Kasha would be forced to crawl into the car as he called her name loudly enough for the other students walking nearby to hear. He knew she was too well-mannered to risk a scene in front of others. He counted on that.

One day, while walking to school and looking frantically for Antoine's car, Kasha was smacked hard on the back by someone. She turned in fear, poised for flight, to look into the face of a young classmate, Audrey. "Wait, Frenchie. How come you're always running from your dad? Why does he always have to force you to take your lunch money and how come you always give it away? Are y'all rich?"

Kasha simply responded, "I hate him."

Audrey had laughed and said, "I wish he'd give *me* money. At least you have a Dad. I wish he was my dad." Kasha remained quiet. Inside, she screamed, "He's not my dad!"

One day, Kasha made it to school without running into Antoine. She quietly hoped that he had skidded in the dirty November snow and smash into a pole and died. That same day, Audrey came to school late and with a handful of quarters. That was how Kasha knew that Antoine had not died in a car accident. Somehow she was not surprised.

He would live forever to torment her.

Audrey never looked at Kasha that entire day, even when Kasha tried to speak with her; and Kasha would have been embarrassed to find out why Audrey had gotten the quarters that day, and many handfuls thereafter. Antoine was more frequently absent from his regular route to cut her off on the way to school. Kasha was grateful that something was keeping him from bothering her those mornings. She began to excel in school and even got better grades than her American peers in English classes.

In the tenth grade in high school, Kasha felt bold enough to ask Peggy if she could meet Henri. "What do you want from him?" "I want a father," she yelled. Peggy looked at her daughter. Kasha had become an attractive, if not beautiful, young girl. She was something Peggy could be proud of, because she got good grades in school, helped with the younger children, and had not caused her further problems with Antoine. Not every child could learn to live with a stepfather, but Kasha was special. She had long ago lost her stutter, but she had become very much like Mimi in temperament. She was rarely seen and she rarely talked or complained, but lately she had begun to hit the younger children and to yell at Peggy when addressed. Peggy figured that the child was getting too old for her to handle alone. Maybe, Henri would take her for a while..."O.K. If you can get another great report card this June, I'll find you his telephone number."

In July of 1975, Kasha was on her second airplane trip. When she had first dialed the Florida number provided by Peggy after straight A's the last marking period, her hands had shaken. Henri had sounded surprised and pleased that she had been able to hold her own in French as they spoke on the phone. He had sent her a round trip ticket. She, in turn, had sent him a photograph. He called back to complain about her afro, that she worked so hard to maintain. "My dear, you are not American. There is no glory in being a black American over being Haitian. Your culture is rich in its history. We may be the poorest nation in the western hemisphere, but that is not forever. There are many of us in exile who are working hard to change that. Do all you can to look and sound

Haitian in order to distinguish yourself from the black Americans. They are hated here in the United States. As for me, I have made it a point never to lose my french accent, just to stay distinct from them. And even though I have been eligible to be a United States citizen for many years, I have retained my own Haitian citizenship. So, get rid of the Afro before you come down her and meet my friends, my dear." Now, as the plane landed, Kasha wondered if all this had been a good idea. She'd wanted so much to impress him and she'd appeared to succeed over the phone. But in person...

Kasha got up and followed the other passengers off the plane. Quietly, she offered up a prayer of thanks that she had not thrown up on this trip. She had never even seen a picture of Henri. Those had all been destroyed long ago by Peggy who feared random searches by the *makouts* after his hurried exile.

Still, from the escalator, she recognized the man who simply had to be Henri. She knew he was at least twenty years older than Peggy, but she was shocked by how old he looked.

He held her away at arms' length and nodded slowly, appraising her. Kasha searched his face fleetingly for signs of disappointment. When Kasha thought that moment would never end, he offered her his cheek for the customary greeting. She kissed him. He'd patted her on the back and exhaled deeply, guiding her out of the airport and into the parking area. That was it. Very perfunctory, and yet the warmest moment that would ever occur between them.

The air outside the airport was warm and humid and smelled of automobile exhaust. He said very little as they drove nearly twenty minutes to a moderate neighborhood in Miami. Kasha couldn't wait to get to know him. She could not believe she was sitting next to her very own father. Things would be different. She wondered if she would tell him about Antoine. No, she could not. he would think her dirty. She needed so badly for him to be proud of her. There would be Christmases and Christmas presents in her future. Peggy had always excused herself from the Christmas ritual with, "Do you really think that a fat white man with a bag full of presents would dare come into this neighborhood late at night? He'd be looking for a serious bruising! No, Kasha, Santa doesn't come by here."

Once she told him how hard she worked at school (She had made sure to pack up the last five years' report cards), he would want to pay for her college expenses also! Maybe he would buy her a car!

She breathed gently, enjoying the smell of her father's cologne. He smelled clean and rich. Not like the sweaty Antoine.

Shortly after leaving the airport garage, they sat in his living room while he told her stories of his life achievements, but he'd always end with: "But, my dear, I have suffered much in my life. I am a very lonely man".

Kasha had listened patiently, sure she'd get a chance to boast also. They had the whole summer. Then, she could hardly believe her ears as he told her of something called prostate cancer and of his two-year struggle with it. "But what are you saying?" "I can't believe your mother didn't tell you. I thought that was why she finally allowed me to see you. I have asked for years, but she refused because she has tried to punish me for not sending for her after my exile. She failed to understand that being a man alone in a strange country was not good for me. I found someone who agreed to be with me, if only to care for the house and for my other God-given needs. How would I know the cow would become pregnant? And once she was pregnant, I could hardly put her out with a child in her belly." "But..." Kasha was not sure how to address him. She was not comfortable with "father" yet and she could hardly call him by his first name. "But, that means you have another wife?" "No, my dear. I have one wife. She is still in Haiti. I am speaking of Natalie, a young malheureuse I was with briefly until she decided she no longer needed me. That's how they have always done your poor father. I take them out of poverty, educate them, teach them so much and then they think they are too good for me and leave. I am a very lonely man, my dear. I prayed that God would allow me to see your face before I die, and now that you're here, I can die, my dear."

Kasha felt herself getting angry. "Don't say that," she said in denial. You will not die."

Kasha struggled with feelings of hate towards Henry for his impending death. Sure he made himself sound as if he had always sought her out, but he was an adult and had not been able to accomplish what she had in finding him. Now, he was calmly letting her know that he would be leaving her again, only this time for good. Only, he made it sound like a simple trip out of town, and not as heavy and final as it was feeling in her heart. She felt guilty for feeling that, and kept it to herself so as not to make him feel guilty about dying. How selfish would he think she was!

Kasha also felt ill at ease about his comments on the women he had known in his life. It seemed that he could only perceive the world from his own perspective. She made herself kiss that soft, wrinkled, coal-black face, the hands with the knotty veins outstanding. She smelled the breath that already stank of death and decay and was content that it did not matter.

She ended up staying in Florida. He had no one. He had just "lost a very selfish mistress a month before you came; and after all the good I have done in my life, I find myself alone...alone!"

Kasha was glad in her heart that he was alone. He needed her. She would not have to go back to Peggy and Antoine. "So that's all that's left to him," she mused to herself. Somehow deep inside she felt satisfied that he was only a part of who he seemed to have been. She felt that she would have been a lot less satisfactory to this man in his better days.

Peggy had not understood her desire to remain in Florida with Henri, but to her credit, had not argued too much about it. "I've got to take all that's left," Kasha told her. "No one else is coming to take care of him. He says they've all abandoned him because he has no money left. I want him to know that I'll be happy with having him for this little bit of time." "What about school?" "School will wait. I'll read a lot. I'm already learning so much about medicine, maybe I'll become a nurse or even a doctor someday."

Kasha waited for a retort from Peggy, but Peggy was silent. Then she said, "Son of a bitch. He is getting what he deserves. He is dying alone." "Okay, good-bye. I'll call again." Kasha delved into the caretaking aspects of Henri's failing health. She walked or took buses to pharmacies to pick up medication. She made phone calls to doctors and hospitals and insurance companies. The summer blurred past. Kasha felt a private sense of selfishness that she was doing for him something that he had never done for her; and she hoped that he felt guilty.

If he did, he never said so.

Five months later, Kasha was in a funeral home in Miami, looking at what was left of her father in a casket. Funny, it didn't resemble him at all. She'd been at the wake for over two hours and had finally gotten the nerve to approach the coffin. She was surrounded by French speaking relatives of Henri's, including the famous Madame Berceuse who seemed to appraise her with some combination of disdain and pity. Peggy had not traveled to Florida for the *occasion* as she had put it. She didn't have to. There were numerous other fair-complexioned women there with children connected to Henri Berceuse by DNA. Even in Miami, the concern for appearances was strong. All were welcomed and hands were firmly squeezed and cheeks daintily kissed.

Kasha saw a young woman who could have been her twin sister, and she wondered at how different life might have been if Peggy had allowed her to meet her father earlier.

But, it had always been the same story from Peggy: "He's no good; If he wanted you, he'd find you. All he ever wanted was women and more women. He can't have you, you're his daughter, so he doesn't need you."

Kasha wondered helplessly what could have happened to Peggy to make her hate Henri so much? She always seemed to miss him when

Antoine was cruel to her, but at other times, she insisted that he was no good.

No one had ever told Kasha that Henri had been dying. She wondered if she'd have searched so diligently or even worked so hard in school over the years to make this unknown father proud.

Now, as she was propelled closer to the casket by the bodies of unknown mourners, she felt no fear as she'd always dreaded. She felt only a deep and empty ravine inside of her that moved up slowly and steadily through her chest and past her throat. "Oh, God," she thought. "I think I'm dying. No, worse, I'm going crazy".

She struggled to keep the noise that filled her head and heart from spilling out to where these virtual strangers who daintily patted their eyes with scented handkerchiefs could notice.

And so the darkness overcame her and she fainted.

Kasha regained her senses on a couch that was strategically placed in the hall of the funeral parlor. The hot tears which washed her cheeks were mirrors to the first time she'd embraced Henri.

Now, as she lay on the couch, she took note that the memories she had of Henri were not the fairy tale types that she had dreamed of creating with him before she met him. Her thoughts were filled with visions of his quickly emaciating body leaning against the bathtub as she wiped his rectum.

He had had to wear diapers during his last days, and she purposely would speak with him in French of things completely unrelated to the task at hand. Sensing her purpose, he would play along, but she would stop making conversation and just spit unobtrusively in the sink between wipes.

When the cancer had ravaged his insides, she had bravely wiped away blood leaking out with the feces, and clenched her eyelids shut and prayed for strength so that she would not vomit or black out. God had answered that prayer.

Funny thing, when she awakened one too many times one night and prayed once again that she would actually pass out and die because she could not take it anymore, God's mercy had not seemed as available. Maybe it was because she had chosen to stay with him.

Kasha thought about going back to New York, to Peggy, to Antoine. She felt that she could tell Peggy about Antoine now. She did not expect sympathy. She still anticipated criticism and punishment, but she didn't care anymore. She felt she could look at Antoine and feel sorry for him, but she reserved the right to hate him forever. She felt even sorrier for Peggy because she knew that her mother could never leave Antoine.

Kasha felt that she could do anything she pleased, and she would. She had finally become something in her life. She had been a daughter to a father, her own father. It had been only for a very short time, but she had a face to go with his name. She could identify a source of her existence, if not the reason for it.

Kasha now felt even hungrier for a father than before she'd met Henri.

It seemed unfair that darkness was much more a part of her life than the light. But she had learned to seek the light; and even if once she had found it, it had drawn back into blackness, she had at least grasped one small ray and coasted far.

She would know how to find it again.